* * * * * * * * * * * * * * * *

THE BEGINNING OF
HEAVEN AND EARTH

THE BEGINNING OF HEAVEN AND EARTH

✳✳✳✳✳✳✳✳✳✳✳✳✳✳✳✳✳

The Sacred Book of Japan's Hidden Christians

TRANSLATED AND ANNOTATED BY
CHRISTAL WHELAN

UNIVERSITY OF HAWAI'I PRESS, HONOLULU

In memory of
Richard de Menocal

© 1996 University of Hawai'i Press
All rights reserved
Printed in the United States of America

96 97 98 99 00 01   5 4 3 2 1

Library of Congress Cataloging-in-Publication Data
Tenchi hajimari no koto. English
The beginning of heaven and earth : the sacred book of Japan's
hidden Christians / translated by Christal Whelan.
p.   cm.
Includes bibliographical references and index.
ISBN 0–8248–1806–7 (alk. paper). — ISBN 0–8248–1824–5 (paper :
alk. paper)
1. Crypto-Christians—Japan.   2. Catholic Church—Japan—
Membership.   3. Japan—Church history.   I. Whelan, Christal, 1954–
II. Title.
BX1668.T4513   1996
275.2'08—dc20   96–12374
CIP

University of Hawai'i Press books are printed on
acid-free paper and meet the guidelines for permanence
and durability of the Council on Library Resources

Book design by Kenneth Miyamoto

✳ ✳ ✳ ✳ ✳ ✳ ✳ ✳ ✳ ✳ ✳ ✳ ✳ ✳ ✳ ✳ ✳ ✳ ✳

Contents

****

Preface

ANYONE SEEKING primary documents written by Japan's Kakure Kirishitan (Hidden Christians) about their experience of persecution will be disappointed. Such documents do not exist. The only works available on the subject are national and local histories. These may contain sections on the Kakure Kirishitan as a historical phenomenon, but they are not written by contemporary Kakure Kirishitan. Although the Kakure Kirishitan have lacked the circumstances or simply the desire to write or rewrite their own history, they did, however, compose one unforgettable work—*The Beginning of Heaven and Earth (Tenchi Hajimari no Koto)*—their sacred tale. But without knowledge and experience of the Kakure Kirishitan, this fascinating and bewildering amalgam of legends and tales is difficult to interpret.

In an effort to understand Kakure Kirishitan religion and society, I adopted an anthropological approach to their study. From September 1991 to August 1992, I spent eleven months in fieldwork among the Kakure Kirishitan in the Gotō Islands. My aim was to live as closely with them as they would permit. Only in this way did I think it would be possible to acquire the necessary keys for interpretation of their complex traditions and sometimes convoluted means of expression.

In my translation of this text, I have utilized the Japanese edition of Ebisawa Arimichi, which is based on the reconstruction of two manuscripts (Zen and Hatakeda). I have opted to leave the

Japanized Latin and Portuguese words as they are in the original text since much of the hybridized spirit would otherwise be lost.

The *Tenchi* is written in Edo-period (1603–1868) Japanese with numerous honorifics. Since to render these into English would be to stultify and distort this folk gospel, I have tried instead to have the text speak in the manner of the Kakure Kirishitan people I have known in the Gotō Islands.

✻ ✻ ✻ ✻ ✻ ✻ ✻ ✻ ✻ ✻ ✻ ✻ ✻ ✻ ✻ ✻ ✻ ✻
Acknowledgments

FIRST I OWE my thanks to the Kakure Kirishitan people who taught me what they remembered of their ancient and vanishing religion. Without their trust and hospitality no research would have been possible. I am grateful to Kimiya and Masaru Yaguchi, who shared their home with me. I wish to thank their daughter, Kaori Iwasaki, who helped interpret the difficult local dialect into standard Japanese for me with uncommon patience and humor. The encouragement and untiring energy of Sister Nakamura, native of Hisakajima, will always be remembered. I owe thanks to Yuka Ogawa, for her varied and relentless support, and to Misako Tanaka of Nagasaki, who kindly helped me with the transcription of taped materials.

I am indebted to numerous scholars at Tokyo University, where I was a research student in Religious Studies in 1993. Peter Knecht of Nanzan University shared with me his vast knowledge of Asian folklore. Constance Krueger offered her invaluable skill in the translation of German articles. I am extremely grateful for the many scholarly and editorial corrections received from Michael Cooper, S.J., of Sophia University.

I owe thanks also to Moselio Schaechter for his generous financial assistance during my first two years in Japan. His kind support greatly facilitated this research on the Kakure Kirishitan.

✻ ✻ ✻ ✻ ✻ ✻ ✻ ✻ ✻ ✻ ✻ ✻ ✻ ✻ ✻ ✻ ✻

Manuscript List

EXCEPTING the Murakami manuscript, this list is based on Tagita's manuscript description in *Kirishitan-sho, Haiya-sho* (Ebisawa 1970b:634).

1. Hatakeda manuscript: dated 1827, received from Fr. Hatakeda Shuhō's friend (name unknown). Origin: Gotō Islands (specific location unknown). Graceful calligraphy and style.

2. Zen manuscript: dated Bunsei period (1818–1830), received from Shimomura Zenzaburō. Origin: Nishi-Sonogi peninsula, Higashi-Kashiyama. Graceful calligraphy and style that appears to be the same hand as MS 1.

3. Yota manuscript: dated Taishō period (1912–1926), possibly written by Yota Matsuo. Origin: unknown.

4. Ichidaiki manuscript: dated 1904, received from Yamaguchi Keizō. Origin: Gotō Islands, Fukuejima.

5. Michiwaki manuscript: undated, received from Michiwaki Masutarō. Origin: Gotō Islands, Narushima.

6. Gen'emon manuscript: dated 1922, written by Matsuo Kyūichi. Origin: unknown.

7. Shimogawa manuscript: dated circa 1889, written by Shimogawa (first name unknown). Origin: unknown.

8. Kyūichi manuscript: dated 1926, written by Matsuo Kyūichi. Origin: Nishi-Sonogi peninsula, Kurosaki.

9. Suke-Jii manuscript: dated 1919, written by Hisamatsu Suke'emon. Origin: Nishi-Sonogi peninsula, Nagata.

10. Murakami manuscript: undated. Origin: Nishi-Sonogi peninsula, Kurosaki. Manuscript still kept in the Kakure Kirishitan community.

****

INTRODUCTION

✲ ✲ ✲ ✲ ✲ ✲ ✲ ✲ ✲ ✲ ✲ ✲ ✲ ✲ ✲ ✲ ✲

The Beginning of Heaven and Earth

FOR WESTERNERS of the mid-sixteenth century, Japan, known then as Zipangu, was a remote country revealed to Europeans through the Far Eastern travel accounts of the Venetian explorer Marco Polo (1254–1325). No European had yet reached Japan, although Polo's hearsay account later earned it fame as a place where "the king's palace is covered with gold" (Mazzali 1982:123). It was Polo's book, too, that had inspired Christopher Columbus to set sail for Asia—not in search of India and its spices but of Zipangu and its gold.

The Portuguese were the first Europeans to arrive in Japan. In 1543, a junk manned by Chinese was blown off course and wrecked upon the island of Tanegashima, located some 20 miles from the southern tip of Kyushu. On board were three Portuguese merchant adventurers. On the shore of this island, and with the assistance of a Chinese crewman as interpreter, the first dialogue between Japan and the West began.

Christianity Comes to Japan

A year after the arrival of the Portuguese, a man from Kagoshima named Yajirō, who was wanted for manslaughter, escaped Japan by concealing himself aboard a Portuguese ship. Placing his hope in the Christian religion, he was baptized in 1548 after his arrival in Goa (Boxer 1966:36). There he studied at the Jesuit College of

St. Paul, where he acquired rapid proficiency in the Portuguese language. With the proverbial enthusiasm of a convert, he is said to have memorized the Gospel of Matthew and to have written it down in Japanese.

The Jesuit missionary Francis Xavier (1506–1552) was impressed by Yajirō, from whom he learned that Japan was ripe for evangelization. Yajirō claimed that if the missionaries' conduct were above reproach, and if they could sufficiently answer the inquiries put to them about the Christian religion, the Japanese would follow reason and convert within six months. With that inducement Xavier set sail for Japan. In 1549, Xavier together with two Spanish Jesuits, Cosme de Torres and Juan Fernández, and with Yajirō as interpreter, arrived in Kagoshima.

Japan at this time, divided into some sixty-six provinces, was ravaged by civil wars. When the missionaries arrived, although the Ashikaga family ruled as shoguns, the country was actually divided into domains and governed by local rulers, or daimyo, whom the missionaries referred to as "kings" owing to their virtual autonomy. In this climate of social instability, and amidst the spiritual decadence of a Buddhist clergy involved in both military forays and politics, the Christian religion and the Western science that accompanied it met with considerable receptivity.

Missionary reinforcements arrived in 1552, and in the course of time more Jesuits came in the trading ships. During the early missionary period in Kagoshima, owing to the fact that the Jesuits and Portuguese merchants who had come to Japan arrived from the south, the Japanese called them *nanbanjin,* meaning "Southern Barbarians." People came from outside the city to hear the preaching of the foreigners from the "homeland of Shaka" (Schurhammer 1982:109). This misperception—that since the Christians had come from India, the religion they brought with them was, in effect, a sect of Buddhism—was partially Yajirō's fault. An uneducated man, Yajirō could not read kanji (Chinese characters), but nevertheless Xavier had to depend on him as a translator and interpreter of Japanese culture. Yajirō, a Shingon Buddhist, had only a superficial knowledge of Buddhism, and he had translated "Deus" as Dainichi

(Buddha Mahavairocana), the supreme deity of the Shingon sect. Thus Xavier, unwittingly, had initially preached salvation through Dainichi. Not until 1551 in Yamaguchi did he realize the error and send Brother Fernández through the streets to tell the people not to worship Dainichi, who was the devil's invention (Frois 1984:1:41).

Apart from religious considerations, missionary activity gradually spread as the daimyo came to see the advantage in offering hospitality to the missionaries. Along with religion came also the impressive Portuguese carracks and the lucrative silk trade with China. The Portuguese could make fortunes as middlemen, exchanging Chinese silks for Japanese silver in the route from Macao to Nagasaki (Cooper 1974:243). The Jesuits also used the intricate bond between commerce and missionary activity to their advantage by urging Portuguese ships to stop only at ports where the daimyo was Christian or allowed the church in his domain. Nagasaki was later to become the main trading depot and was transformed by the presence of the missionaries and the Portuguese carracks from a small fishing village to an international trading center.

Always receptive to the most expedient means of converting souls, Xavier observed a tendency in the Japanese to emulate Chinese civilization in matters intellectual and aesthetic. Buddhist clergy, with whom he had numerous discussions, also suggested to him that Christianity would have greater appeal if it entered Japan via China as previous cultural innovations such as Buddhism and the kanji system had done in the past. Reasoning that the conversion of China would likewise be imitated by the Japanese, Xavier left for China in 1551, although he died the following year without reaching the mainland.

Missionary activity expanded. By the 1560s a Christian community was also established in Kyoto, but Kyushu still remained the center of Christianity and the site of the Jesuit *seminarios* (preparatory schools) and numerous churches. The success of the religion was partly due to the conversion of the daimyo of Ōmura, Bungo, and Arima. It often happened that the subjects of a daimyo followed their lord's example, and this accounted for the phenomenon of mass conversions and helps explain some of the surprising baptism statistics for such a small band of missionaries. In 1553, with only five missionaries in the country, the total number of converts in three separate regions reached approximately 4,000 (Schütte 1968:428; Frois 1984:1:66–70). By 1579 converts to Christianity numbered 100,000 although there were only fifty-five missionaries in the whole of Japan (Schütte 1968:429, 321).

The Christian religion continued to flourish for about fifty years after its introduction. It enjoyed particular favor under the protection of the warlord Oda Nobunaga (1534–1582), whose use of the Portuguese gun had given him a distinct advantage and helped him to begin the unification of his war-torn country. Nobunaga's generosity toward and alliance with the missionaries were at least partially due to the leverage it gave him against the powerful militaristic Buddhist sects. With the death of Nobunaga in 1582 and the rise of Toyotomi Hideyoshi (1536–1598), the unification of Japan was nearly completed by 1590.

Initially showing favor toward the Christian religion, Hideyoshi was to turn against it after a visit to Kyushu, where he witnessed for himself the extent of the religion's influence. In July 1587 Hideyoshi issued the first edict against Christianity: it declared the expulsion of the foreign missionaries from Japan within twenty days of its issuance. This ban was not strictly enforced, however, and the missionaries continued their activities, although with a measure of discretion.

The Jesuits had enjoyed being the sole missionary presence in Japan for thirty years; the papal brief *Ex Pastoralis Officio* (1585), issued by Pope Gregory XIII, guaranteed the mission of Japan exclusively to the Jesuits. In spite of this, the Jesuits were soon joined by other missionaries: the first Franciscan mission was established in 1593, and the Dominican and Augustinian missions followed suit in 1602. The arrival of the three friar groups marked the beginning of bitter rivalry and territorialism, particularly fierce between the Jesuits and the Franciscans.

The efforts of the Jesuits in the field of education were remarkable. With the aim of forming a native clergy, Jesuit *seminarios* had been established in both Arima in Kyushu and Azuchi near Kyoto in 1580. The students for these schools were young boys recruited from the upper levels of society. Their curriculum included the reading and writing of Latin, Japanese, singing, and music. The first *collegio*, or college, was also established in the same year in Bungo, where students studied philosophy and theology.

For these institutions of Christian education, appropriate textbooks were necessary. In 1591, the Jesuits established a printing press with movable type. This press was brought to Japan by the visitor of the Jesuit mission to the Orient, the Italian Alessandro Valignano (1539–1606), known for his advocacy of missionary adaptation to local culture. Avoiding all controversial works, the Jesuits printed devotional books, translated religious classics such as the *Guia do Pecador* (Sinner's Guide), and rewrote popular works such as *Esopo no Fabulas* (Aesop's Fables). In addition, they published catechisms, liturgical calendars, and dictionaries in Japanese, Latin, and Portuguese. A grammar, *Arte da Lingoa de Iapam* (1604–1608), by João Rodrigues may be the first scientific study of the Japanese language (Cooper 1974:235).

The missionaries' efforts were soon to be compromised by an unfortunate incident that would aggravate relations between the Jesuits and Franciscans. In 1596, a Spanish galleon from Manila, the *San Felipe*, on its way to Acapulco, was blown off course by a typhoon. Laden with a rich cargo, it foundered off the coast of Shikoku and its cargo was seized by local officials. This action sparked bitter protests involving both the Franciscans and the Jesuits, and the controversy resulted in Hideyoshi's turning his wrath against the Christians. In fact, he ordered the crucifixion of all Christians in Kyoto. The original list was in the hundreds but sympathetic officials reduced it to twenty-six. In 1597, six Franciscans, three Jesuits, and seventeen laymen were crucified in Nagasaki. These victims later became known as the Twenty-six Martyrs.

After Hideyoshi's death, Tokugawa Ieyasu (1542–1616) was victor at the Battle of Sekigahara in 1600 and the virtual ruler of Japan. Three years later Ieyasu's rule became official when he was made shogun. Ieyasu continued the unification begun by his two predecessors. It was at this time that repercussions of the defeat of the Spanish Armada (1588) began to be felt in Japan: Spain and Portugal now had formidable competitors with the arrival of the Dutch traders in 1609 and the English traders in 1613. Ieyasu, who had tolerated the missionaries in order to maintain the lucrative silk trade, now had other options. The Portuguese gradually lost their exclusive trade privileges with the Japanese to these Protestant newcomers, with whom it was possible for the Japanese to trade without the complication of missionary activity.

In 1614 an edict proscribing Christianity was issued. In this edict, Japan was described as "the country of gods and of Buddha." It condemned the Christian religion as the opponent of Confucian morality, Buddhist law, and the Shinto way—the amalgam that constitutes the Japanese religious temperament. Not only did it demand that daimyo send any foreign missionaries in their domain to Nagasaki for deportation, but it also ordered the destruction of all the churches. The native Christians, too, were compelled to recant their faith, and prominent Japanese Christians were sent into exile in Manila or Macao. Those who did not comply were subject to "divine punishment."[1] This edict was a measure intended to completely eradicate the foreign religion from Japan. Although many Christians accepted martyrdom rather than deny the faith, others opted to conceal their religion. This edict, then, may be considered the beginning of the clandestine Christian tradition.

Many missionaries left Japan, some went underground, and still others, disguised as traders, continued to enter Japan smuggled aboard Portuguese ships. In an accelerated effort to extirpate the Christian religion, in 1636 the Portuguese traders were confined to a diminutive fan-shaped island connected by a bridge to Nagasaki. Called Dejima or Deshima, this island was constructed specifically for these traders, with the purpose of restricting their contact with the Japanese population to inhibit any infiltration of Christianity.

But Christianity received its severest blow in the wake of the Shimabara Rebellion (1637–1638), an uprising on the Shimabara peninsula of Kyushu, a place where Christianity had deep roots.

This rebellion stemmed from the profound anger of the overtaxed farmers in the Matsukura domain. It was a local policy to arrest the wife and daughters of any farmer unable to pay his taxes. During one such incident in which a father watched his daughter tortured, he killed the daimyo's stewards in a burst of rage. Other villagers rose up in his defense, and the resistance of this band of rebels became a movement that spread across the region to include neighboring Amakusa. The rebellion soon assumed a much wider significance. The rebels carried a flag with the Portuguese motto *Louvado Seia o Santissimo Sacramento* ("Praised be the Blessed Sacrament"). It is easy to understand how this rebellion was interpreted as a Christian liberation movement, and was treated as such. The revolt was put down only after a great struggle. The insurgents and their families, numbering about 40,000, occupied the abandoned Hara castle, where they were massacred.

The authorities were thoroughly alarmed by the challenge of this insurrection. As a consequence, trade with the Portuguese was completely severed in 1639 and contact with the West was limited to the islet of Dejima. Confined here were traders in the employ of the Dutch East Indies Company, who alone were permitted residence in Japan.

Underground Christianity

At the beginning of *sakoku,* or self-imposed national isolation, an estimated 150,000 Christians had gone underground. The practice of *e-fumi* (trampling on Christian images) began around 1629 as a means of detecting Christians by observing who would shrink from the act.[2] It was later systematized with the establishment of the Shūmon Aratame Yaku (Religious Inquisition Office) in 1640, whereby the ceremony was integrated into the new year's celebrations in temples throughout Kyushu.

Another institution, the *gonin-gumi* (five-family group) system of mutual responsibility, was introduced to keep the general populace in good order. Accordingly, the misdeeds of a single family member would have consequences for all. Although this policy was intended to intimidate the faithful from practicing their religion, if all five families were Christian, practice of the religion was virtually guaranteed to go undetected. In fact, this system was actually one of the institutional mechanisms that, ironically, appears to have helped to preserve Christian community life by facilitating the formation of an underground network (Kataoka 1974:20). This was possible because the structure of the *gonin-gumi* corresponded with the organization of the religious sodalities and confraternities already established by the missionaries. The sodalities were groups of men, women, and children who met periodically for retreats and spiritual discussion and to inform the remaining missionaries of safe hiding places. The confraternities were devoted primarily to works of charity.

The Franciscans and the Dominicans, in particular, had a long tradition of establishing Third Orders—small monastic bands of men and women who led lives of devotion without taking vows. The friars established such groups in Japan and they served to keep the religion intact. The Franciscans initiated the Confraternity of the Cord; the Dominicans established the Confraternity of the Rosary; the Jesuits founded the Sodality of the Blessed Virgin (Ebisawa 1960:291). When the central government began its persecutions, these groups constituted the religious core of the community in the absence of the priests.[3] The members worshiped together, prayed together, and offered mutual support.

The Christians lived under constant threat of persecution, according to which harassment and torture were deemed successful if they induced apostasy. Some punishments designed for this purpose were the retraction of employment (which inevitably led to begging or starvation), dismemberment, branding, water torture, lowering the victim's body into the boiling sulfur springs of Unzen, and the *ana-tsurushi,* or headfirst suspension in a pit of excrement until the victim either recanted or died.

In 1680, when Tokugawa Tsunayoshi (1646–1709) became the new shogun, the brutal attitude toward Christianity manifested itself in the change of kanji used to write the word for Christian in Japanese. The word for Christian was pronounced "kirishitan," based on the Portuguese word *Cristão*. According to the *Nihon Kirisutokyō Rekishi Daijiten* ("Japanese Christian Dictionary"), the original kanji used was 吉利支丹. Without literal meaning, the original kanji suggested both happiness and prosperity. But the first character used in *kirishitan* was one that Tsunayoshi also used to write his own name. As he objected to any character in his name being used in connection with the odious religion, he thus had the characters changed at that time to the ones still used today: 切支丹. This new compound can be interpreted as "to cut the limbs until they bleed." One other compound was sometimes employed: 鬼理死貪. This may be rendered as "a demon's ideology hungry for the dead."

In this climate the Kakure Kirishitan (Hidden Christians), the descendants of Japan's first Christians, continued to practice what they remembered of the Catholic faith. Although the Bible had never been translated into Japanese, devotional books containing all the major Catholic prayers in Japanese with sprinklings of Latin and Portuguese had once circulated. The faithful had already committed some of these prayers to memory. Nevertheless, their knowledge of their new religion is highly questionable given the missionary strategies of the time. Because the missionaries believed that salvation was impossible without baptism, they adopted the "extension method" of conversion. This meant that they opted for breadth at the expense of depth. They baptized as many people as possible with the minimal amount of indoctrination: this instruction, they believed, could be deepened at a later date (López Gay 1966:11–36).

But this second stage never had a chance to develop sufficiently. Besides the constant threat of persecutions, the missions suffered from a chronic shortage of priests: in fact, the number never exceeded 137—to administer to a congregation of 300,000 at its height.[4] Most believers had probably received only about ten days of instruction in the faith. Thus those who went underground probably were not able to distinguish clearly between Buddhism and Christianity. And this lack of distinction would have intensified over the long years of covert practice as the Kakure Kirishitan wove together, unintentionally, Buddhist cosmology with Christian mythology. The amalgam of eclectic spirituality the Kakure Kirishitan practiced they also defended as *Christian*. Despite the impediments to religious freedom, the underground Christians established their own religious hierarchy, observed holy days, and administered baptism.

Discovery of the *Kakure Kirishitan*

With the arrival of Matthew Perry and his "black ships" in 1854, Japan's isolation finally came to an end, and the Treaty of Amity and Commerce (1858) permitted Americans to practice their religion in Japan. Similar agreements were made with other countries, encouraging missionaries who were once again eager to enter Japan. The Catholic church, hoping to avoid the rivalry between diverse missionary groups that had characterized the earlier era, granted exclusive rights to the conversion of Japan and Korea to the Société des Missions-Etrangères de Paris. French missionaries went to Okinawa as early as 1844 to study Japanese and wait for the reopening of Japan and permission to preach.

While waiting to enter Japan, in fourteen years the French missionaries had managed to baptize only two Japanese, and one of these baptisms had actually taken place in Hong Kong. By 1859 two French priests had entered Japan, although the anti-Christian edicts were still in effect. One of these, Fr. Prudent S. Gerard, accompanied the first consul general of France as interpreter and chaplain. The Japanese consented to the construction of Christian churches, but these were to administer to the needs of foreign residents only.

The Catholics established churches in Hakodate, Yokohama, Edo, and Nagasaki. Father Gerard, the first superior of the mission between 1858 and 1866, had heard that some Hidden Christians, the remnant of the church that Xavier had founded, lived in remote mountains. A few had only recently been put to death. He wondered how many more might still be hiding, and he hoped that his mission might make contact with these descendants of the ancient

Christians (Marnas 1896:336–337). This was also the hope of those missionaries who began to work in Nagasaki, where Christianity had once flourished in the sixteenth and early seventeenth centuries.

The discovery of the Kakure Kirishitan on 17 March 1865 by the French priest Bernard Petitjean (1829–1884) has been told so many times that its meaning has gravitated from history to legend. While it is typical to speak of Petitjean's "discovery" of the Kakure Kirishitan, the reverse is perhaps a more accurate description of the event, since it was the underground Christians who first approached Petitjean. Father Petitjean's diary entry for that day relates how fifteen Japanese were waiting at the door of his newly built church on Ōura slope in Nagasaki.[5] Three women then knelt beside him and said, "The heart of all of us here is the same as yours." Then they asked, "Where is the statue of Maria-sama?" (Marnas 1896:488). These words opened a new era, for now Petitjean knew that he was in the presence of the Kakure Kirishitan.

Although this encounter of the French priest with the Kakure Kirishitan is well documented, what has continued to remain hidden is the fact that Petitjean was the first person outside the circle of Kakure Kirishitan to receive a copy of their bible, a work known as the *Tenchi Hajimari no Koto* (Beginning of Heaven and Earth). This text was given to Petitjean on 14 April 1865 by Domingo Mataichi, a *mizukata* (baptizer) from Urakami. Mataichi claimed that his manuscript had been written from memory in the years 1822–1823 (Tagita 1978:77–78). Petitjean was deeply impressed by Mataichi, who was not only able to recite from memory the Salve Regina and other Christian prayers, but knew the Catholic baptismal formula in words still recognizable as Latin: *Kono hito wo paotizo in nomne Patero, Hilio, et S'ra Spiritou Sancto, Iamoun* ("I baptize this person in the name of the Father, Son, and the Holy Spirit. Amen.") (Marnas 1896:506).

Petitjean took this precious manuscript with him when he resettled in Yokohama. In 1874, however, a fire destroyed the Missions-Etrangères de Paris residence there and with it the printing press, religious items, and, it seems, that early manuscript of the

Tenchi. Commenting on the text, Petitjean had once said: "We have found in it some errors, but they are of little importance" (Marnas 1896:507). He was most likely referring to elements in the *Tenchi* unrelated to Christianity. Not all clergy would have agreed with his estimation, however. In 1931, when Bishop Urakawa was asked about the whereabouts of the manuscript, he said that some years previously Father Salmon of the Nagasaki diocese had examined it and found it "worthless" (Tagita 1966:2:136).

Although it is impossible to know with precision the contents of that exemplar, Petitjean decided that the *Tenchi* would serve as an excellent model for a catechism he intended to write for the underground Christians then emerging. The lexicon of the *Tenchi,* with its many Portuguese and Latin words, was evidence of the Iberian tradition the Kakure Kirishitan had long nurtured. Petitjean, extremely sensitive toward the Kakure Kirishitan, understood that their recognition of what was Christian depended on its expression in terms of an Iberian lexicon within a Japanese framework. By imitating both its structure and lexicon, Petitjean eventually wrote his catechism: *Seikyō Shogaku Yōri* (Fundamental Catechism of Christian Doctrine).

When word of the missionaries' return to Japan spread throughout Kyushu and its offshore islands, for some it seemed the fulfillment of one of four prophecies of the local martyr Bastian—*Basuchan no yogen* (Bastian's Prophecies)—which promised that the priests would return in black ships (Kataoka 1979:559). Petitjean estimated the total population of Kakure Kirishitan then emerging to be around 10,000. This estimate seems excessively low, for the number eventually reached closer to 50,000, of whom only about half actually rejoined the Catholic church.[6]

Unlike Catholic priests who were later to work in the Nagasaki area, Petitjean was impressed by the Kakure Kirishitan's knowledge of Catholic theology: they knew of the Trinity, the Fall, the Incarnation, and the Ten Commandments. Without books or priests to instruct them or renew their faith, they had transmitted several prayers orally and many knew the Lord's Prayer, the Hail

Mary, the Apostles' Creed, the Confiteor, the Salve Regina, and the Act of Contrition.

Petitjean recounted a visit to Shittsu in Sotome, a region northwest of Nagasaki, in 1865. During his overnight stay, he went to a home in which the family had preserved a picture depicting the fifteen mysteries of the rosary, with pictures of Saint Francis of Assisi, Saint Anthony of Padua, and a third unidentified saint at the base.[7] People in the village gathered to worship in the home that kept this holy picture. Moreover, the usual religious organization he found at that time consisted of two principal officials: the first—the *chōkata* (calendar man)—was a man who could read and write and whose duty it was to lead the Sunday prayers and administer to the dying; the second official was the *mizukata* (baptizer).

Tagita Kōya: Rediscovery and Research

The pioneering research of Tagita Kōya (1896–1994) was the next significant contact with the Kakure Kirishitan. His work revealed for the first time the complexity of the situation and the unusual psychology of the Kakure Kirishitan, who preferred to continue practicing their religion in secret despite religious freedom.[8] Tagita discovered the Kakure Kirishitan accidentally while researching his thesis, "The Religious Mentality of Japanese Schoolchildren." When he sent eight thousand questionnaires to schools throughout Japan, some of the responses surprised him. In one district the words "purgatory," "heaven," and "hell" often appeared as responses to the question: "Where do people go when they die?" The word "purgatory" especially aroused Tagita's curiosity, and he went to visit the area—Iōjima, a small island off the coast of Nagasaki. There he discovered that 90 percent of the population were descendants of the first converts to Christianity in the sixteenth century (Tagita 1965:152).

This particular group had rejoined the Catholic church, and Tagita began to search for more Catholic villages like it. In the course of his search, Tagita discovered the Kakure Kirishitan, who had refused to reunite with the Catholic church since the return of the missionaries in the 1860s and the freedom of religion granted in the Meiji Constitution. They preferred to continue their own form of worship informed by the spiritual fragments of the Iberian Catholicism they had inherited from their ancestors.

Why had these people continued to hide or at least to insist on their separate identity?[9] This problem was the beginning of Tagita's extensive ethnographic fieldwork. Throughout the 1930s, Tagita was engaged in research in and around Nagasaki, in Sotome, in the Gotō Islands (an archipelago in the East China Sea, west of Nagasaki), and in Ikitsuki and Hirado (islands off the coast of northwest Kyushu). These were all areas heavily Christianized in the sixteenth and seventeenth centuries, and many communities of Kakure Kirishitan were still to be found there intact.[10] When I met Tagita in 1992, he spoke of the difficulties of his research at a time when roads were few and the only way to travel in those remote areas was on foot or by boat. His energy and tenacity of purpose brought him into close contact with many communities. In 1931 a ninety-one-year-old man of Kurosaki in Sotome, named Monsuke, recited the *Tenchi* from memory for Tagita. This was Tagita's first contact with the *Tenchi* narrative (Tagita 1978:77).

In the wake of that encounter, Tagita searched diligently for manuscripts of the same work. Through his long and tactful acquaintanceship with the Kakure Kirishitan, he managed to acquire nine exemplars of the *Tenchi Hajimari no Koto*. He then turned his attention to the scholarly community, to whom he introduced this hybrid narrative of the Kakure Kirishitan that melded together Buddhism, Christianity, and folk religion and customs into an imaginative whole. Between 1955 and 1962, Tagita gave more than three hundred lectures in the United States, Europe, and India. The first edition of his *Shōwa jidai no sempuku kirishitan* (Secret Christians of the Shōwa Era), published in 1954, contained a version of the *Tenchi*. Since that time, however, knowledge of the Kakure Kirishitan and their fascinating gospel appears to have remained confined to the field of Christian scholarship in Japan. Only within the past few years has the *Tenchi* begun to come into its own and attract the serious attention of scholars in disciplines as various as linguistics, psychology, and folklore.

Kakure Kirishitan Sectarianism

Contemporary researchers of the Kakure Kirishitan have often been puzzled by the sectarian nature of these religious communities. This is a feature that the missionaries of the reemergence period (1860s) observed as well. The interpretation of Meiji-era missionaries is of great interest, since their contact with the Kakure Kirishitan was made when the tradition was more intact. These missionaries observed that different communities used different names in reference to themselves—Kirishitan, Bateren, and Dogio—according to whether their original teachers were Franciscans, Jesuits, or Dominicans. Moreover, the saints they revered and the feast days they observed differed from group to group. In a chapter that deals with the discovery of the Christians, Francisque Marnas relates how the first Christians to reveal themselves to the missionaries appeared to belong to the Franciscans, since they preserved the prayer known as the Confiteor with invocation to Saint Francis along with the apostles Peter and Paul (Marnas 1896:565).

Since the early Christian period in Japan was characterized not only by bitter conflicts but also by rivalry among the missionary groups themselves, especially between the Jesuits and the Franciscans, the missionaries' distrust of one another may ironically have been transmitted as part of the Kakure Kirishitan tradition itself. If close alliance with one particular Catholic religious order is a major reason for their sectarianism, the Kakure Kirishitan today have no recollection of this motivation, although they maintain a stance quite inflexible toward compromise with other villages. Religious vocabulary, saints' days observed, vows, modes of worship—all vary from village to village, although only two basic styles of ritual, known as *shimokata* and *kamikata,* exist.[11] Apart from these historical considerations, whether traditionally Kakure Kirishitan or Buddhist-Shinto, villages in Gotō are usually composed of relatives and tend to be rather closed and cohesive units.

Within the village unit, mutual dependency and cooperation are the rule, but to extend this policy beyond the village confines would require a special reason such as marriage.

Even though the Kakure Kirishitan are now faced with dwindling numbers and a lack of successors, unification is still viewed as a disagreeable option.[12] Attempts to unify on an islandwide basis have failed on the Gotō Islands of Narushima and Fukuejima (Whelan 1992:385; 1996:122–137). At present, the ancient religion appears to be evolving in the direction of assimilation into neighboring religions.[13] Tempukuji, a Buddhist temple located in Kashiyama in Sotome, offers a good example of this trend. According to Shioya Hidemi, the eleventh-generation priest at Tempukuji, when he began extensive restoration work on the temple in 1978, the number of families in his register increased from 180 to 250. This was because 70 Kakure Kirishitan families joined that year. For many the meaning of their own religion had become ever more tenuous and their long familiarity with a temple that did not antagonize them made the switch to Buddhism a natural step. "The Kakure Kirishitan had wanted to change their religion for some time," says Reverend Shioya. "The restoration of the temple merely provided them with a good occasion to join." All 250 families willingly donated 80,000 yen toward the project.[14]

The *Tenchi*'s Genealogy

The text of the *Tenchi* published here is divided into fifteen chapters with an approximate length of 14,300 letters—kanji and hiragana (phonetic cursive script). Evidence suggests that the *Tenchi* originated in Sotome—the original homeland of the Kakure Kirishitan groups of the Gotō Islands who emigrated to Gotō in the 1790s (Whelan 1992:382). Of the nine exemplars that Tagita collected, three are from Sotome and three are from the Gotō Islands: one from Narushima, one from Fukuejima, and one from an unknown location in Gotō. The origin of the remaining three manuscripts was evidently not written on the manuscripts, but philologist Kojima Yukie has reconstructed the manuscript genealogy and determined that they too come from Sotome (Kojima 1969:72).

Aside from these nine manuscripts, another version from Sotome was copied down in 1976 and later published in *Nagasaki Dansō* (Topics on Nagasaki; 1994) by Diego Yūki, S.J. The undated autograph copy, however, is still kept by the Kakure Kirishitan leader of a group in the Kurosaki area of Sotome. A total of ten versions, then, are the only ones that have surfaced to the present. (See the manuscript list on pages xi–xii for details.) Since all known manuscripts of the *Tenchi* are from either Sotome or the Gotō Islands, this work is considered a distinguishing feature that separates their tradition from that of the Kakure Kirishitan of the islands of Ikitsuki and Hirado.[15]

The *Tenchi* was first published in *Katorikku-shi* (Studies in Catholicism), where it appeared in four installments in 1938–1939. This publication was based on the Zen (Shimomura Zenzaburō) manuscript, using the Kyūichi and Gen'emon manuscripts for collation. In 1932, Tagita sent a copy of the Kyūichi manuscript to Alfred Bohner, who translated it into German and published it in 1938 in *Monumenta Nipponica*. Tagita then republished the Zen manuscript in his monumental work on the Kakure Kirishitan, *Shōwa jidai no sempuku kirishitan* (1954). He considered this manuscript the most graceful in style and calligraphy and believed that it contained the fewest lacunae. He used the Gen'emon manuscript for its collation. In 1966, Tagita republished the Zen version in *Nagoya joshi shōka tandai kiyō* (Journal of Nagoya Women's Junior College of Commerce) (Tagita 1966–1967:3–4). In this work he included his own literal English translation with the original Japanese on the facing page. In 1970, Ebisawa Arimichi and others (1970a) published an authoritative edition of the *Tenchi* with an ample commentary in *Kirishitan sho, Haiya sho* (Kirishitan and Anti-Kirishitan Writings). This edition was based on the Zen manuscript with the use of the Hatakeda manuscript for collation.

The *Tenchi* manuscripts are written predominantly in either hiragana (phonetic cursive script) or katakana (phonetic block script) with a minimal use of kanji. The responsibility for writing

was usually delegated to the *chōkata,* the highest-ranking member
in the tripartite hierarchy of the Kakure Kirishitan, or to the next
in rank, the *mizukata.* The infrequent use of kanji in the texts
serves as evidence of the low level of literacy among the Kakure
Kirishitan.[16] Moreover, all the *orassho* (Lat. *oratio:* prayer) books I
have seen in the Gotō Islands are written in katakana, even in cases
where their owners have independently achieved a level of education that permits them to read newspapers and write the basic
kanji. This situation is probably due to the fact that today it is difficult to know how to transcribe the prayers, part of an oral tradition, into kanji. Transcription from a phonetic system (kana) to a
semantic one (kanji) requires a clear understanding of meaning.
This semantic gap is one of the most serious problems impeding
the transmission of the Kakure Kirishitan tradition in recent years.

Theory of the *Tenchi*'s Origin

The *Tenchi* continues to challenge scholars who have attempted to
interpret the text and understand its function in the Kakure Kirishitan communities. Is it really the bible of the Kakure Kirishitan
or merely a collection of old stories, a long folktale, or perhaps the
remnant of a sixteenth-century Christian mystery play written and
performed in Japan?[17] When was this work, originally part of an
oral tradition, first written and why? What might have served as a
model for the *Tenchi*? And what function, if any, does it serve
among the present-day Kakure Kirishitan?

The *Doctrina Christan,* a work first published by the Jesuits in
Amakusa in 1592, clearly had left an indelible impression in terms
of its lexicon on the minds of those who created the *Tenchi.* Perva-
sive use of Portuguese and Latin is a feature preserved in the *Tenchi*
narrative. The *Doctrina,* written in the form of questions and
answers between master and disciple, also included all the fundamental prayers a Christian of the sixteenth century was expected to
know. The *Tenchi,* although it mentions these prayers by name,
does not actually include them. Might the *Tenchi* have served a
function for the underground Kakure Kirishitan like that of the

Doctrina Christan for the early Kirishitan?[18] Given the prolonged secrecy of the Kakure Kirishitan groups and the waning memory of traditions such as the *Tenchi* today, no definitive answer seems possible.

Philologist Kojima Yukie's efforts to determine the origin of the *Tenchi* are worthy of discussion here.[19] In a statistical study (Kojima 1969) of the vocabulary in the text, based on an analysis of the Zen manuscript, she compares the *Tenchi* with nine works published by the missionaries in Japan, six from the sixteenth and seventeenth centuries and three from the Meiji era. Kojima's analysis reveals that of all the texts with which the *Tenchi* is compared in the "Christian century"—the early period of Japanese-Portuguese contact—except for the *Doctrina Christan,* the *Tenchi* has the highest percentage of loanwords. Unlike the loanwords in the *Doctrina,* which are doctrinal terms, those in the *Tenchi* consist of toponyms and personal names. If these are subtracted, the statistics for the *Tenchi* closely resemble those of *Esopo no Fabulas* (Aesop's Fables; 1593). The *Esopo* and the *Tenchi* have almost the same number of verbs, adjectives, and frequency of native Japanese words. This last characteristic accounts for the colloquial style common to both works. Moreover, the *Tenchi* resembles the Jesuit *Heike Monogatari* (Tale of Heike; 1592), a work containing no foreign words, in that both the *Tenchi* and the *Heike* contain nearly the exact same number of Buddhist terms.

Certain questions then arise from Kojima's linguistic statistics: When was the *Tenchi* composed? Who composed it? What was its function, since it was written in a colloquial style approximating that of *Esopo no Fabulas* and the *Heike Monogatari?* Kojima is convinced that the *Tenchi* originated in a heavily Christianized area, for its knowledge of Buddhist concepts is extremely superficial. Although the *Tenchi* and the *Heike* share the same number of explicitly Buddhist terms, the *Heike* is permeated with Buddhist sentiment whereas the content of the *Tenchi* is predominantly Christian.

The lack of understanding of the European foreign words (Veronica, for example, is "Agnus Dei") and the use of *ateji* (purely phonetic use of kanji) discount the possibility of foreign authorship and suggest for Kojima that the work was composed at a time when no missionaries who might correct such errors were left in the country. She surmises that after all the missionaries had left Japan, the remaining Christians formulated the *Tenchi*. This would be in the latter half of the seventeenth century. The raw ingredients of the *Tenchi*, however, were taken from discussions between missionaries and the faithful in the latter half of the sixteenth century. When traveling to a new area, the missionaries were accustomed to preach by telling stories from both the Old and New Testaments. These encounters may be considered the germ of the *Tenchi*.

The century that elapsed from the formation of the story to its written form was sufficient time for the many "errors" to enter the tradition. The pictorial language and the colloquial style of the *Tenchi* reveal that it probably was not originally intended to serve dogmatic purposes, but existed rather as a story meant to delight its listeners. When Deusu addresses his angels concerning the sorry plight of humans, for example, he uses a familiar and unelevated tone: "Oh, anjo, look here. What can I do? How can I help them?" Initially, then, the *Tenchi* was most likely a collection of old stories and not a sacred scripture at all. The fairytale quality of numerous episodes supports this conjecture: as the fugitive Holy Mother and her son wander the lands, she weaves clothes for him from spiderwebs. The story of Maruya and the King of Roson (Lucon) is yet another example. That scene may also have provided a dramatic catharsis for a group of people severely oppressed by the rich and powerful. The image of Pappa Maruji's lame son—carried over the sea on the back of a lion-dog statue come to life—is a symbol of hope for the weak and abandoned. All of these stories transport the listener into the realm of the fantastic, magical, or supernatural.

Kojima's thesis is logical with respect to the germ of the *Tenchi*. But rather than the notion of an original text, whether oral or written, undergoing a process of degradation with errors slipping in over time, it might also be argued that many Christians were probably not sufficiently indoctrinated from the beginning—that is, "errors" may have existed even with the missionaries still in the country. The chronic understaffing of the missions, coupled with the scattering effect of the persecutions, is likely to have disrupted steady contact between the priests and their converts. Whether these "errors" existed from the start or crept in over time and under isolation would depend on the amount of sustained contact between the missionaries and those who created the *Tenchi*.

There is another problem, however, and this regards the evolution of the *Tenchi* as a text. Why would the *Tenchi* have evolved from an oral tale, meant to delight and edify, into a sacred scripture? The very first sentence in the Murakami manuscript advises the reader to raise the text above the head as a sign of deference before reading further. In Japan this gesture is appropriate when receiving a gift and before reading a sacred text or handling a religious statue. The reverent attitude of the Kakure Kirishitan author or copyist toward the text indicates that at a later phase the *Tenchi* did acquire a more serious and sacred function in the communities that possessed a copy. The *Tenchi,* then, would seem to have evolved from an engaging tale into a sacred book for the Kakure Kirishitan at some stage in the past. This shift in attitude may have marked the initial impulse to commit the tale to writing—in other words, the transition from an oral to a written tradition. With the mission-aries absent and the Catholic religion a crime punishable by torture and death, the *Tenchi* was perhaps the last and only link with Christianity.

It is possible, therefore, that the *Tenchi* began as a pleasant story or chant, but later, owing to the dearth of Christian materials, it assumed, from sheer necessity, a more dogmatic role. It was necessary to give structure to a religion in danger of disappearing. The explicit reference to the three groups of religious mysteries of the rosary, in terms of a textual division into morning, noon, and night sections, suggests that the *Tenchi* might have served as inspirational reading at communal prayer or rosary gatherings. The times of the day for gathering and the meditations assigned to each are all delineated in the *Tenchi*. Nevertheless the *Tenchi,* a collection of the wisdom of the Kakure Kirishitan people, still reads like a long and complex folktale that weaves together theology and folktales of Eastern and Western origin and attempts to reinterpret and justify Japanese customs in terms of its own interpretation of Christianity. In other words, the *Tenchi* tries to Christianize the native Japanese elements, and succeeds in Japanizing Christianity. For this reason the best definition of the work might be to call it indigenous theology, a folk gospel, or a Japanese Christian apocryphal text.

On 23 August 1994, I interviewed the present owner of the Murakami manuscript, who is the leader of a Kakure Kirishitan village in Kurosaki. He stated that his community does not use the *Tenchi* at all nor can he recall it ever being used; he himself considers it a strange and incorrect work. By this, Murakami is referring to the *Tenchi*'s native elements—such as the episode of the boys who paint the lion-dogs' eyes red or the justification for the custom of women shaving their eyebrows and blackening their teeth. Instead of using the *Tenchi* as their primary religious text, this Kakure Kirishitan man's village uses the *Doctrina Christan* of 1600 edited by Ebisawa Arimichi and published in 1950. For this leader, the prayers of the *Doctrina* are complete and correct, and its contents represent the true religion of the *kyū-kirishitan* (ancient Christians), which he and his community still practice.

The reason for Murakami's detachment from the *Tenchi* in terms of religious practice reflects a situation common to other contemporary Kakure Kirishitan: the result of contact with a range of non-Kakure Kirishitan people. Kurosaki Church was built in 1920 and as Murakami began to have more contact with Catholics, he became increasingly self-conscious about his identity as a Kakure Kirishitan. One example that illustrates this trend is a calendar he made showing all contemporary Catholic feast days and Kakure Kirishitan feast days in parallel lines. Murakami says that he was interested in discovering if the two religions had anything in common. These comparisons revealed overlapping feast days, he affirms, and relativized his own position as a Kakure Kirishitan. Contact with the outside was also responsible for Ebisawa's edition of the *Doctrina Christan* finding its way into Kakure Kirishitan hands.

Murakami's impulse to research his own tradition and its relation to Catholicism, along with his comments, imply that the *Tenchi* expresses a diminished or distorted form of Christianity better substituted by the more orthodox *Doctrina*. In recalling Father Petitjean's positive assessment of the *Tenchi*, it is useful to recall that he and Father Salmon held contrary views and did not equally esteem the text. Rather than imagine that the text itself continued to evolve into something less Christian, it is more likely that one priest judged it according to its similarities with Christianity and the other in terms of its departures. In this way, both assessments might be considered correct, according to each man's point of reference.

Murakami claims that his grandfather alluded to the *Tenchi* as the work of a *biwa hōshi*—a tale chanted by a wandering musician to the accompaniment of a *biwa* (four-stringed Japanese lute). Other villagers in Kurosaki also claim to have heard the same theory of the *Tenchi*'s origin from local people now deceased. The early transmission of the *Tenchi* to various Kakure Kirishitan communities through a wandering minstrel is an intriguing possibility, but it cannot be substantiated without more evidence.

Watching the documentary *Kanashimi no Agari Itsu: Nagasaki no Kakure Kirishitan* (When Is Easter?: Nagasaki's Kakure Kirishitan), produced for television in 1984, afforded me a special insight into the problem of origins and transmission among the Kakure Kirishitan. In this program, Murakami and his now deceased father are featured in their home displaying the autograph copy of their *Tenchi* manuscript. While the camera focuses on the text, the voices of father and son are heard in the background. One of them states that Yanagita Kunio had once expressed his view that the *Tenchi* was a *biwa monogatari* transmitted by a wandering minstrel. But what the younger Murakami told me ten years later omitted any mention that this was the opinion of Yanagita Kunio. In ten years the voice of an outside authority had become the voice of Kakure Kirishitan tradition itself.

This substitution of an outside interpretation of tradition and history in place of a local one is a recurring pattern among the

Kakure Kirishitan. On 11 October 1995, I visited a Kakure Kiri-
shitan official on Narushima who had recently replaced a *mizukata*
who had died the previous year. He spoke about his history as a
Kakure Kirishitan and referred to the missionaries who came to
Japan in the sixteenth and seventeenth centuries as "Americans."
The Tokugawa Bakufu had ultimately made "the Americans" leave
Japan. Other than this original touch, the version he told could be
found in any national history book and contained nothing local.

Another instance of substitution and confusion of traditions
occurred during my fieldwork in 1992. The town hall informed an
elderly Kakure Kirishitan *mizukata* that a foreign historian visiting
Japan wished to discuss the *Tenchi* with a Kakure Kirishitan. This
was the first time the elderly *mizukata* had ever heard of the work,
and both he and the town officials, afraid of losing face, consulted
a Catholic sister on the island, who advised the old man to read the
Book of Genesis in the Bible. He was given a Bible and copied the
entire Book of Genesis into his own notebook and then titled it
"Tenchi Hajimari no Koto."

Although it no longer seems possible to discover a single origin
of the *Tenchi,* one can gain insight into the thought processes of
the Kakure Kirishitan by observing the way they continue to re-
construct origins through the assimilation of various currents of
thought available to them. Numerous scholars, writers, and missionaries have visited the islands over the years since Tagita made
the existence of these communities known through books, newspapers, magazines, lectures, film, and even television broadcasts.
The result of this contact has been a "loss of innocence" or at least
a rupture in the continuity of transmission. The consequent flood-
ing and confluence of various streams of thought into the Kakure
Kirishitan psyche now pass for "tradition."

This is perhaps a recurring phenomenon that has long per-
sisted. Recent historical contact with Americans in World War Two
is blended with Tokugawa history. In similar fashion the *Tenchi*
itself was probably formed from stories once heard by missionaries
and then mixed with more local concerns. Thus we have tales such
as the King of Roson's proposal to Maruya (Virgin Mary). Likewise, rumors of the importation of human mummies for medicine

led to a meditation on the implications of ingesting the flesh of another human.

Time and evolution did not degrade the Christian message in the *Tenchi;* rather, the attitude of the Kakure Kirishitan toward the text and their own tradition has been radically transformed over the years. Contact with outsiders has created terms of comparison hitherto unthinkable and has generated competing versions of history and truth. Comparisons with texts and new knowledge from the dominant culture have caused the gradual diminishment of the *Tenchi* and its loss of status as a canonical work.

On several occasions Kakure Kirishitan have spoken with humor about encounters with Catholic priests or students of theology who told them that their *orassho* did not make sense even in Latin. Before their rediscovery, Kakure Kirishitan could esteem their traditions and texts unself-consciously, regardless of whether they understood them; today, however, Kakure Kirishitan are confronted with a world of competing values in which their own tradition has been assigned to the periphery.

The reverence with which Murakami continues to regard the *Tenchi* is not diminished by the fact that the text no longer has the status or function of scripture. The *Tenchi* was the spiritual sustenance of his ancestors, among whom it enjoyed a privileged status. It is a tangible link with the past. As Murakami affirmed during my interview: "If it weren't for the *Tenchi,* Christianity would have completely died out in Japan." This statement may appear hyperbolic, but it also reveals Murakami's sense of integrity. Although he has no use for the *Tenchi* in his community of worshipers, he recognizes its historical importance for his ancestors, whose options were more limited. The *Tenchi* once served as sacred scripture, a status it has since lost in the community. Despite his earlier criticism of the text, this Kakure Kirishitan's gratitude for the function it served is clear.

Christian, Buddhist, and Folk Influences

The *Tenchi* is a compilation of Christian legends, a fusion of Buddhist and Christian cosmology and theology, as well as myths explaining the origin of many Japanese customs interpreted in light of a divine plan allegedly held to be Christian by the Kakure Kirishitan. From a universal religion such as Catholicism, the *Tenchi* constructs a local universe and a local religion entirely Japanese in spirit.

The syncretism of Buddhist and Christian traditions in the *Tenchi* is notable and reminiscent, too, of the earlier commingling of Buddhism and Shinto known as *honji suijaku*. Accordingly, the Buddhist deities were considered as fundamental or original *(honji)* and the Shinto deities *(kami)* as their manifestation *(suijaku)*. A similar sort of Buddhist-Christian coexistence is revealed in telling phrases like this one: "As for the one you worship as Buddha, he is called Deusu, Lord of Heaven. He is the Buddha who introduced the salvation to help humankind in the world yet to come."

A reader approaching the text for the first time is initially surprised by a few of its idiosyncracies. Certainly one encounters chronological leaps—such as Adam and Eve, after eating the apple, prostrating themselves before God and offering the Salve Regina (a prayer to the Virgin Mary, not yet born). There is geographical confusion as well—such as the impossibly long trek Mary would have had to make in traveling from the Kingdom of Luçon (Philippines) to Bethlehem (Israel). And, too, there is personification—such as Sacrament as a person descending from heaven to tutor Christ in Catholic theology.

The narrative opens with a genesis account, but it swiftly shifts to the New Testament with no mention of the other parts of the Old Testament or knowledge of Jews, Judaism, and Christ's identity as a Jew. While only the names of prayers and not their content are recorded in the *Tenchi,* a copy of the *Go-passho* (Passion Prayer) referred to in Chapter 10 was obtained from the Kakure Kirishitan at another time by Tagita (1978:145). As this prayer mentions the Jewish people, some notion of Jews as a group must have existed at least in some communities, although the Jewish people are placed in contraposition to Christ in the prayer.

The Christian contents of the *Tenchi* predominate and are derived from three sources: biblical stories, popular Christian legends, and apocryphal stories. The biblical events depicted are the creation of heaven, earth, and humans, the fall of the angels and Eve and Adam, the degeneration of humankind, the flood, the arrival of a savior, the story of Mary, the life of Christ, the death and ascension of Christ, heaven and its saints, the hereafter, and the apocalypse. A purgatory story is also included at the end of the work. The loose organization of the text and the brevity of the chapters impress the reader as a compilation of various stories rather than an organically conceived narrative. This seems particularly clear with the closing of the text—a purgatory story, which has no particular reason for being the last page of the work. This rather open-ended structure of self-contained chapters gives the whole text the quality of a work in progress from which it is possible, if not to delete, at least to interpolate portions. The nonbiblical Christian elements derive from popular medieval miracle legends such as Our Lady of the Snow, Christ and the Wheat Sower, and the Cross Tree. Other stories are found in Christian apocryphal sources—the detail of the succoring animals that surround Christ at his birth, for example, and the names of the Three Magi.

A dominant Christian structural influence on the narrative is the Catholic rosary. Of the missionary groups in Japan, the Franciscans and the Dominicans were particularly devoted to the rosary. The Jesuits, however, published a detailed book on the rosary, *Supiritsuaru Shugyō* (Spiritual Exercises; Nagasaki, 1607), with blockprints depicting each of its fifteen mysteries. The Dominicans likewise published a lengthy book on the subject at the height of the persecutions. Titled *Virgen S. Maria no Tattoki Rosario* (Precious Rosary of the Holy Virgin Mary), it was published in Manila in 1622. It appears that each missionary group introduced the rosary to its converts, furnished them with rosary beads, and taught them the accompanying meditations.

The creation narrative of the *Tenchi* is followed by the life of Mary and Jesus. The episodes narrated are those corresponding to the fifteen mysteries of the rosary that outline the lives of Mary and Christ: the five joyful mysteries, the five sorrowful mysteries, and the five glorious mysteries. This division refers to the three separate sittings a day in which devout Catholics traditionally said the rosary while meditating on the events it represents. While all fifteen mysteries are included in the *Tenchi*, the last five are given less vivid treatment—probably because they are the most abstract and the Kakure Kirishitan have little tolerance for abstraction.

Buddhist elements can be seen in the concept of ranks and forms. Major characters in the *Tenchi*—Deusu, Maruya, Jusuheru —are described in terms of rank. Actions, too, determine rank as can be seen when Maruya refuses the King of Roson's proposal. She travels to Deusu in her flower wagon, and having pleased Deusu by proof of her vow of chastity, receives a rank before descending to earth. The description of the numerous heavens recalls Buddhist cosmology despite the Christian names assigned to these realms. Terms such as *gokuraku* (Buddhist paradise) and *naraku* (Buddhist hell) stand alongside purgatory and limbo. The delightful fusion of Christianity and Buddhism is seen when those who have received baptism are said to follow Deusu to Paraiso, where "it is guaranteed that they will all become buddhas and know unlimited fulfillment for eternity."

Folk religious elements are found in the concept of assigning lucky names to people. It is a popular custom in Japan for someone oppressed by misfortune to change names in hopes that luck will also take a turn for the better. Consider the intriguing figure of the lame son of Pappa Maruji. The boy, abandoned by his father before the great flood because he is crippled, suggests the *hiruko* of Shinto myth and popular devotion to Ebisu as the returned *hiruko*. The incestuous marriage between Chikorō and Tanhō recalls other consanguinous unions such as that of Izanagi and Izanami.

The *Tenchi* has no function at present in the Kakure Kirishitan communities of the Gotō Islands. After Tagita collected Michiwaki Masutarō's copy of the *Tenchi* of Nagahai village in 1931, knowledge of the narrative on Narushima seems to have passed into oblivion. With one exception only—on Fukuejima—no Kakure Kirishitan informant, including officials in their nineties who were interviewed, had ever heard of it. While the *Tenchi* may be unknown as a "text," stories from it are often part of local lore. I once had occasion to meet a Kakure Kirishitan woman on the small island of Kabashima who spontaneously told me the legend of the wheat sowers, which I had already encountered in the *Tenchi.*

Indigenization of Christianity

The *Tenchi* reveals much about Japanese cultural history, not from the tip of the pyramid, but from the mouths of those habitually silent and excluded from history. It rises from the deep currents of folk culture in which the Kakure Kirishitan have always lived. The present commentary with its notes on the *Tenchi* is an attempt to disclose as much as possible of Buddhist theology, Japanese customs, and Catholic traditions and legends in the way they might have been practiced by the Japanese in the sixteenth and seventeenth centuries. In fact, Catholic tradition when seen through Kakure Kirishitan eyes assumes a surprising beauty and fascination. Mary is no statue on a pedestal but an earthy, intelligent, and shamanistic girl of twelve. She too becomes one of the persons of the Trinity. The entire paternal Judeo-Christian tradition is turned gracefully on its head and feminized. This orientation owes much to the fact that the *Tenchi* originated in an agricultural society, a structure that typically fosters fertility or earth cults.

Worldwide such cults affirm the primacy of nature in the form of a Great Mother who contains all seasons; she issues typhoons and avalanches, but also roses and sunshine. In any event, she requires worship and propitiation. Judeo-Christianity originated as a sky cult among a nomadic people whose God is rational and the creator of nature. But the repressed image of this powerful Great Mother, from whom life arises and is likewise crushed, springs up in various guises when Christianity sinks its roots in rural areas dependent on agriculture. In popular Catholicism in Europe, the figure of the Great Mother reappears in certain forms of devotion to the Virgin Mary in the countryside. In his book *Madonnas That Maim* (1992), Michael Carroll documents numerous cases of Virgin apparitions in Italy of the fifteenth century during which Mary left her devotees crippled and maimed as a sign of her power. The reemergence of the raw and irrational force of "chthonian nature," to use Camille Paglia's apt term, is precisely the power that is most often suppressed as paganism. Christianity has never succeeded in either eradicating or converting this force. The Christian response has inevitably been to idealize brotherly and sisterly love, or *agape,* a concept based on the acceptance and cultivation of a defused or all-encompassing love object. But this gentler form of love finds a formidable opponent in the focused and insatiable force that characterizes the chthonian in all its diversity.

To adopt another framework, novelist Endō Shūsaku has long popularized the idea of paternal and maternal religions as *chichi* (father) and *haha* (mother) religions (Endō 1941:153–165; 1994: 206–211). These refer respectively to the religious temperaments of Oriental and Occidental people. Accordingly, we witness a shift from *chichi* to *haha* in the Christianity of the *Tenchi*: Eve is not made from Adam's rib but is an independent creation. This is probably because indigenous Japanese religion locates symbolic power in the feminine: in Shinto mythology, Izanami is a Great Mother. Later Amaterasu-Ōmikami, Japan's solar goddess, from whom the imperial line is said to descend, is born. She is the supreme deity of the Shinto pantheon and the prototype of all *miko* (spirit mediums). Female shamans have always been closely associated with the sun in Japanese tradition.

The character of Mary is that of Great Mother and shaman. She fits into the seemingly contradictory and archaic pattern of "virgin-fertility." It is thus no surprise that Mary is the strongest and most developed character in the *Tenchi*. Her virginity, while allegedly Christian chastity, has much in common with the pagan derivation of the Christian virgin birth: "The Great Mother is a virgin insofar as she is independent of men" and thus "symbolically impenetrable" (Paglia 1990:43). Is Mary in the *Tenchi* likewise a madonna that maims? She clearly rejects the king's advances and causes his chilling death. Is her later compassion for the deceased king another attempt to Christianize the more brutal instincts?

One of Christianity's great strengths is that it can be shaped in the image of whatever society adopts it. But at what point within the dynamic of acculturation does a separate sect come into being? The transformation of foreign elements in the *Tenchi* inevitably occurs when the concept introduced by the Christian missionaries has no cultural bedrock on which to rest in Japan. Concepts introduced to them, such as the Trinity, were either never fully digested or they resisted understanding what did not appeal or seem relevant to them.

Another difficult concept for these early Japanese Christian converts was clearly that of original sin. Although Adam and Eve sin by eating the fruit, the idea of this fundamental sin is not sustained and drops out of the narrative to such an extent that the very reason for Christ's crucifixion is called into question. In fact, Christ does not appear altogether innocent in the *Tenchi*. If not patently guilty, he is at least responsible for the slaughter of the 44,444 innocents who died in his place while he and his mother fled. This appears to be the reason why he must be crucified, and he too understands his imminent crucifixion and death in these terms. In view of these fundamentally non-Christian concepts, Father Petitjean's comment about the *Tenchi* containing "errors of little importance" might best be attributed to his excessive enthusiasm, since these are indeed significant departures from Catholic doctrine.

A Hybrid Cultural Heritage

The *Tenchi* is a work of folk literature and a cultural product of collective authorship. This means that its function in the community is neither context-free nor stable. Its early context was in all likelihood the encounter between a storyteller or a *biwa hōshi* and a community of Kakure Kirishitan listeners. Their response had an editorial function insofar as listeners determined both the story selection and its ultimate meaning (Raz 1992:36–37). The *Tenchi*, then, was continually adapted to the needs of the Kakure Kirishitan communities at different times. The remnant of a Christian mystery play, a collection of old stories, a long folktale, a holy bible—it probably served all of these functions at some point in the past, just as now it has been rendered meaningless by the same community that once treasured it.

How did the *Tenchi* lose its function in the Kakure Kirishitan community? When the *Tenchi* crossed the barrier from "insider" to "outsider"—from Mataichi to Petitjean, from Monsuke to Tagita, and from Tagita to a world of scholars and writers—it opened up communication between these isolated communities and the rest of Japan and the world. One consequence of this dialogue with the outside was an increased self-consciousness and reflection on communal identity. Even the name "Kakure Kirishitan" was learned from contact with the outside, since all evidence suggests that these groups traditionally called themselves and their religion by no name at all.

The *Tenchi,* a work bred in an insulated environment with an internal logic suitable to those communities, became vulnerable to extraneous commentary and criticism based on reference points of the dominant culture and its authoritative version of Japanese history and Christianity. Opening the *Tenchi* to the outside has diminished its importance for the community through a gradual shift in the locus of meaning away from the local. The end result is a gap between the Kakure Kirishitan and their own ancient traditions. Today their vulnerability is visible in their readiness to accept extraneous interpretations of their own history and experience.

Instead of the *Tenchi,* the Gotō Islands now have television. On stormy nights when squid fishing is too dangerous, a fisherman can always head for the local *sunakku* (bar) or *pachinko* (pinball) parlor. *Orassho* recitations have given way to village gatherings around *karaoke* machines. This is a description of the times, not a judgment of them or nostalgia for the past. Social change has hit the islands and the impact has been tremendous, rapid, and disruptive to the traditional patterns of religion and work in these small fishing communities. Television has exposed them to a national identity in which they can most fully participate if they move to one of its metropolises. This has resulted in a further loss of meaning on the local level and an outflow of the population. The gradual encroachment of mainstream cultural values into the Kakure

Kirishitan mindscape has replaced the insider's perspective with the outsider's and left the Kakure Kirishitan standing outside looking in at their own tradition as strangers. Many Kakure Kirishitan now offer similar critiques of their own culture that one might hear anywhere in Japan. This is what makes Murakami's stance so extraordinary, for he is a man negotiating with dignity between two cultures.

Very few "insiders" are left. In other words, the *Tenchi* has become an artifact on the cultural scene, unknown for the most part to the very group that created it. Even so, the *Tenchi* is the only text the Kakure Kirishitan produced that can represent in a spirited way their hybridized cultural heritage. This highly imaginative text, therefore, seems the best vehicle through which to introduce the Kakure Kirishitan people.

****

THE BEGINNING OF
HEAVEN AND EARTH

❊ ❊ ❊ ❊ ❊ ❊ ❊ ❊ ❊ ❊ ❊ ❊ ❊ ❊ ❊ ❊ ❊ ❊

1. The Beginning of Heaven and Earth[1]

IN THE BEGINNING Deusu was worshiped as Lord of Heaven and Earth, and Parent of humankind and all creation.[2] Deusu has two hundred ranks and forty-two forms,[3] and divided the light that was originally one, and made the Sun Heaven, and twelve other heavens. The names of these heavens are Benbō or Hell, Manbō, Oribeten, Shidai, Godai, Pappa, Oroha, Konsutanchi, Hora, Koroteru, and a hundred thousand Paraiso and Gokuraku.[4]

Deusu then created the sun, the moon, and the stars, and called into being tens of thousands of anjo just by thinking of them. One of them, Jusuheru, the head of seven anjo,[5] has a hundred ranks and thirty-two forms. Deusu is the one who made all things: earth, water, fire, wind, salt, oil,[6] and put in his own flesh and bones. Without pause Deusu worked on the *Shikuda, Terusha, Kuwaruta, Kinta, Sesuta,* and *Sabata.*[7] Then on the seventh day Deusu blew breath into this being and named him Domeigosu-no-Adan, who possessed thirty-three forms. So this is the usual number of forms for a human being.[8]

For this reason the seventh day of one cycle is observed as a feast day.

Deusu then made a woman and called her Domeigosu-no-Ewa,[9] had the man and woman marry, and gave them the realm called Koroteru. There they bore a son and daughter, Chikorō and Tanhō,[10] and went every day to Paraiso to worship Deusu.

One day while Deusu was away, Jusuheru seized the opportu-

nity to deceive the anjo and said, "As I'm also like Deusu, worship
me from now on." Hearing this, the anjo worshiped him saying,
"Ah, behold, behold!"

Ewa and Adan then asked, "Isn't Deusu here?" But Jusuheru
replied swiftly saying, "The Lord is in heaven, but because I am
like Deusu, tens of thousands of anjo revere me. Therefore, Ewa
and Adan, you too worship me—Jusuheru!"

Ewa and Adan listened and discussed the matter between
themselves scrupling, "But we are supposed to worship Deusu."
Just at that moment Deusu, descending from on high, came to that
very spot where they were discussing the issue. The anjo who had
worshiped Jusuheru, and Ewa and Adan, were all startled by
Deusu's sudden apparition. They clasped their hands, and bowed
their heads until they touched the ground. In acknowledgment of
their error they demonstrated their remorse by offering the Konchirisan.[11]

Deusu then spoke, saying, "Even if you should worship Jusuheru, don't ever eat the fruit of the *masan*."[12] And turning to Ewa
and Adan, "If you bring your children to me, I will give them aus-
picious names." Having heard Deusu's most merciful words, everyone returned home together. But Jusuheru, after he heard all this,
rushed ahead to Koroteru with the sole intention of deceiving Ewa
and Adan. Along the way, he got hold of the fruit of the forbidden
masan, and went to Ewa and Adan's home. "Where's Adan?" he
asked, and Ewa answered, "He's out just now guarding the gate of
Paraiso."

Jusuheru continued, "I am Deusu's messenger. Because it is
Deusu's will to bestow lucky names on your children, hurry and
send them to Deusu." Ewa listened and believed. "Thank you for
taking the trouble to come all this way to tell me that," she said,
and paused fascinated. "And by the way, what is that medicine you
are holding?" "Oh, this," said Jusuheru. "It's the fruit of the
masan."

Ewa was surprised and said, "But I hear that fruit is against
our law here in Paraiso. Is it permissible to eat of it?" Jusuheru,
answering with a patent lie, said, "The fruit of the *masan* is some-

thing that belongs to Deusu and to me, Jusuheru." He then added, "It is forbidden because whoever eats it will then obtain the same rank as Deusu."

Ewa listened and asked, "Is that really true?" Then Jusuheru, triumphing over Ewa's doubts, handed her the fruit of the *masan*. "Eat this if you please, my good woman,"[13] he said encouraging her, "and obtain the same rank as I, Jusuheru."

Ewa felt glad as she took the fruit in her hands. With both hands she raised the *masan* above her head in a sign of deference, drew it close to her, and then ate of it. "You should have Adan eat some, too," Jusuheru said, and reminding her of his mission added, "And take your children to Deusu soon." Pretending to be a messenger on his way back to Deusu, Jusuheru hid himself in order to watch what would happen next.

When Adan came home, Ewa told him the story and showed him the fruit she had set aside for him. When she handed it to Adan, he had some doubts but took it in his hands anyway and ate it. At that moment, how eerie it was, for a voice as if from nowhere spoke out: "Adan . . . whhhy? That is the evil fruit." It was the voice of Deusu, and Adan, shaken, stood transfixed in amazement, but no matter how hard he tried to vomit up the fruit it remained lodged deep in his throat.[14] What a pitiful sight it was, for Ewa and Adan too lost the glory of heaven and were transformed on the spot. They offered the Salve Regina,[15] cried out to heaven, and bowed to the ground. Tears of blood flowed from their eyes, and although they had a thousand regrets it was no use.

This incident is the origin of the Contrition *orassho*.[16]

After some time had passed, Ewa and Adan turned to Deusu and implored, "Please let us taste again the glory of heaven." Deusu listened and answered them, "If that is your wish, you must repent for more than four hundred years. Then I will invite you to Paraiso. But you, Ewa, will become a dog in Middle Heaven." Ewa was then kicked and disappeared to who knows where.[17] "As for you, children of Ewa, you must live on the earth, eat beasts, and worship the moon and the stars, and repent. At some later time I will show you the way to heaven."

On the earth there is a stone called *gōjaku*, Deusu told them. If you discover its whereabouts and live in that spot, something miraculous is sure to happen. The place Deusu was referring to is the very place where we are living.[18]

Now Jusuheru, who had hidden himself from Adan and Ewa earlier, was a dreadful sight to behold for his nose had grown long and his mouth wide. His arms and legs had sprouted scales, and horns jutted up out of his head.[19] He bowed before Deusu and said, "It is all because of my evil heart that I have become like this. When I consider my destiny I become frightened." He then begged Deusu, "Please, let me have the glory of Paraiso again."

But Deusu answered, "Oh, malignant one. You will never be the stuff for heaven, and because Ewa's children are doing penance on the earth, it is not possible for you to stay there either. Therefore, you will become the god of thunder." Jusuheru then earned the rank of ten forms and was allowed to reside in Middle Heaven. But, alas, all the anjo who had worshiped Jusuheru, every last one of them, was transformed into a *tengu* and sank down to Middle Heaven.[20]

※ ※ ※ ※ ※ ※ ※ ※ ※ ※ ※ ※ ※ ※ ※ ※ ※

2. The Evil Fruit Cast to Middle Heaven

DEUSU THOUGHT that the fruit of the *masan* was an evil thing for both heaven and earth, so he sent it to the *tengu* residing in Middle Heaven. Ewa's children departed and met in the vicinity where they had discovered a lode of *gōjaku*. Then straight from heaven a naked sword came hurling down. It flew to earth piercing the ground in that very spot where the two had gathered. This was the miraculous deed that Deusu had foretold, and both Chikorō and Tanhō stood silent in great awe. The woman, Tanhō, without thinking hurled a needle that pierced the chest of the man and blood gushed out. Then the man in turn hurled a comb at the woman, and brother and sister thus broke their blood tie, and became man and wife.[21] From then on woman became submissive to man, and the couple took a vow of fidelity. Seeing that all things foretold came to pass,[22] they coupled and had many children.

Since that time the number of humans increased at a steady pace so that food was in short supply. Turning their faces to heaven, the people prayed, "Please, give us food." While they were praying, Deusu appeared in the open sky and gave them rice seeds. They planted these seeds in the fallen snow and in the sixth month of the following year, they reaped a bumper harvest: eight ears of rice produced eight *koku* of rice. The secondary crop produced nine.

This is the origin of the Sowers' Song, "Eight *Koku* for Eight Ears."[23]

Agriculture spread at this time through fields and up into the hills until the food supply became abundant. But the world took a turn for the worse since evil and greed held sway. Three beings were unleashed and entered the world at this time: Ambition, Covetousness, and Selfishness. To satisfy their greedy desires, they stole food from righteous people. Deusu, despising those three, bound them together into a single bundle that bore three faces, and horns sprouted from all three. They were dreadful to look upon, and Deusu said to them, "You selfishly grabbed things that grew in the rice paddies and the fields all for yourselves. I, Deusu, have therefore come down from heaven in order to make you demons of a lower heaven." So saying, he kicked them to the bottom of the sea.[24] These three scoundrels, by the way, were also the doing of Jusuheru.

As the population grew again gradually, people followed the evil precedent set by these three wicked ones: Ambition, Covetousness, and Selfishness. Everyone stole and people were relentlessly greedy and inclined toward evil. Although evil deeds increased by steady degrees, Deusu took compassion on the people and sent an oracle to Pappa Maruji, the ruling monarch of that land: WHEN THE EYES OF THE LION-DOG OF THE TEMPLE TURN RED, A GREAT TSUNAMI WILL COME AND DESTROY THE WHOLE WORLD. Since the time that the monarch Pappa Maruji received this oracle from Deusu, he visited the temple every day to pay his respects to the lion-dogs.[25]

One day while Pappa Maruji was making his customary temple visit, a group of young children gathered around him and one asked, "What's the reason you worship these lion-dogs?" Another child, hearing his reply, relayed it to the others: "When the eyes of the lion-dogs turn red, this world will be swallowed up by a big wave." On hearing this, one of the children laughed his head off, saying, "What kind of silly business is this? We could easily paint them red ourselves, but it's too dumb to think the world will be destroyed." Thus the children went ahead and painted the eyes of the lion-dogs red.

As was his custom, Pappa Maruji set out to visit the shrine the next day. When he saw the vermilion eyes of the lion-dogs a shock ran through his body. He brought out the canoe he had prepared in advance, and made his six children get into it. But because his eldest son was lame, with remorse he nevertheless left him behind.

Then suddenly a huge wave shook both heaven and earth, and within a blink not a spot of dry land could be found, only the surface of the vast sea was visible as far as the eye could see. But over the surface of the sea one of the lion-dogs came running, and on its back it was carrying the lame son who had been left out of the canoe.[26]

In six hours' time, when the tide withdrew, Pappa Maruji together with all of his children made themselves at home on Ariōshima where the lion-dog had also delivered the eldest son. Thousands of people drowned in that wave. They fell to a place called Benbō, a hell of the previous world.

❊ ❊ ❊ ❊ ❊ ❊ ❊ ❊ ❊ ❊ ❊ ❊ ❊ ❊ ❊ ❊ ❊

3. The Division of Deusu's Body for the Salvation of Humankind

THOSE SEVEN whose lives were saved in a timely way by boarding the canoe decided to settle down and make Ariōshima their home. But eventually they had no way to distinguish married persons from single ones.

Thus, the practice of married women shaving off their eyebrows and blackening their teeth began at this time.[27]

As before, the population grew steadily but everyone who had been born and died up until this point had necessarily fallen into Benbō. Deusu felt pity and said, "Oh, anjo, look here. What can I do? How can I help them?" Deusu's anjo answered, "Deusu, if you but divide your divine body, that is a sure way to save them." Taking to heart the anjo's advice, Deusu split into two, and became also the divine son, Hiiriyo-sama.[28]

For this purpose an anjo named San Gamuriya was then sent down to earth as a messenger of Deusu. Later, in the middle of the eighth month, San Jiwan the water official was also sent to earth and lodged in the womb of Santa Izaberuna.[29] The following year, in the middle of the fifth month, when Izaberuna was fifty-three years old, she gave birth to San Jiwan.

Because of the age at which Izaberuna gave birth, one round of *orassho* consists of fifty-three prayers.[30]

In the country of Roson where King Sanzen Zejusu reigned,[31] a girl of humble birth by the name of Maruya also lived.[32] Since her seventh year, she had set her heart and soul on the pursuit of learning.[33] By age twelve she had made great strides and reflected thus: "When I consider the state of our world, I wonder how I can be saved in the world to come now that I have been born into the world of humans." As she thought relentlessly about this, how mysterious it was when she received this heavenly oracle: IF YOU MARUYA WILL REMAIN SINGLE FOR YOUR ENTIRE LIFE LIVING THE ASCETIC LIFE OF A BIRUZEN,[34] I WILL QUICKLY GRANT YOU THE SALVATION YOU SEEK. Much amazed and rejoicing, the girl Maruya threw herself to the ground and worshiped.

Because Maruya received this oracle at age twelve, this is the origin of one round of *orassho* consisting of twelve prayers.[35]

The sovereign of the Kingdom of Roson was searching his lands for a queen. Although much care went into the selection of the candidates, not a single one the king met suited his taste. But when word of the humble Maruya, a girl who lived in his very kingdom, reached the king, straightaway he sent his chief retainers to her home. There in that humble abode they related to Maruya's parents the story of the king's search for a suitable bride.

The girl's parents acted with much deference, and without any reservations accepted the retainers' proposal, saying: "Your wish is our command." In spite of their easy acquiescence, Maruya did not allow her consent at all. The retainers, discerning how things stood, thought they had better not leave matters unsettled in this way. They seized Maruya against her will and brought her before the royal presence. The moment the king saw Maruya, he grew happy and said, "She is even more beautiful than what I have heard." Turning to Maruya, he added, "From now on obey me."

Maruya listened and answered, "Although your wish is reasonable enough, as far as relations between us are concerned, because of my overwhelming wish to be saved, I have already made a vow of chastity and can never have a man." The king hearing this said, "Whatever your greatest wish may be, I will let you have it. So please, be my wife."

Maruya answered saying, "Your Majesty's rank is lower than my humble one, for yours is the splendor of this world alone. But this world is only an inn. The salvation of the next world is what is essential."

The king rebuked her. "You are of humble birth—what rank have you? I have the rank of a king, and have things to show you besides. Come along now, come this way!" Then he drew out many things from his treasure trove: gold, silver, great capital in rice, to say nothing of the gold brocades and ten square *ken* of scarlet silk, precious stones of coral, an incense box of lapis lazuli, objects crafted of agate and amber, incense of *kyara* and musk, and *jinkō*.[36] With clouds of incense wafting through the palace and surrounded by his treasures, the king said, "You will live in a palace inlaid with gold and silver and perfumed with incense, and I will let you have all these things if you just submit to me."

Without so much as a glance at the king's treasures Maruya responded, "Your treasures are temporary and pertain to an ephemeral present. Once you have used them up, they are useless. But now I will show you my secret arts." Turning her face to the heavens above, pressing her palms together and gathering all her

force to the center of her being in prayer, the girl Maruya worshiped and invoked while these words flooded from her: "Reveal
to us your mystery and power this instant."

Her prayer must have reached heaven, for in a short while a
small offering stand, laden with food, appeared before her. When
those present saw this, from the king down to his least subject, all
were stupefied. The king finally broke the silence and said, "Indeed
I've seen marvelous things today and should like to see more."

Maruya listened to the king's words with an air of profound
respect, and once again she turned her face heavenward and
uttered a prayer. Although it was the middle of the sixth month,
the hottest season in that Kingdom of Roson, how awesome to see
the clouds in the sky suddenly gather in dense bunches and the sky
darken a shade. Then delicate flakes of snow began to fall lightly,
and after a short while snow had piled up several feet high.[37]

The king and all those who happened to be present felt their
bodies grow so cold that they could open neither their eyes nor
mouths, and in their astonishment they could not move. During
this interval in which everyone stood in dumb amazement, a flower
wagon came down for Maruya, and she rode away up to heaven
in it.[38]

This is the way the Biruzen Maruya ascended to heaven.

❊ ❊ ❊ ❊ ❊ ❊ ❊ ❊ ❊ ❊ ❊ ❊ ❊ ❊ ❊ ❊ ❊

4. The King's Death

WHEN THE GENTLE snows had ceased to fall, the mental state of the
King of Roson was close to dementia. He felt as if he were waking
from a dream and kept murmuring, "Maruya, where have you
gone? Maruya ... Maruya." Although the king searched for the
girl Maruya, she had already gone up to heaven and there was no
way to see her anymore. But the king continued to long for her so
much and so pitifully that at last in this state of bewilderment and
yearning he died.

Meanwhile, Maruya had reached heaven immediately in the

flower wagon. There she prostrated herself before Deusu, who looked at her and asked, "Biruzen Maruya, how is it that you have come here?" Maruya took in Deusu's words and narrated the story of the King of Roson. Hearing it Deusu rejoiced, saying, "Welcome, welcome indeed. Now I will let you have a rank and title." And Deusu named her "Santa Maruya of the Snow." Right after receiving this new name and rank, Maruya descended from heaven and returned to her original home in the Kingdom of Roson.

One day while Maruya was reading a book, words appeared mysteriously on the page to announce that the Lord was presently to descend from heaven. She paused, wondering where the Lord of Heaven would descend, when suddenly San Gamuriya Arikanjo was sent down from heaven.[39]

Kneeling before the Biruzen Santa Maruya, the anjo said, "The Lord of Heaven is due to descend to earth, so please let us use your young and fresh body for the purpose." Maruya answered, "How marvelous indeed. Just as I was sitting here wondering where he might come, you have come to tell me that it is to me he will come." She was exceedingly glad and assured the anjo, saying, "Your wish is my command." The anjo added, "In the middle of the second month the Lord will come to earth, so please comply with this favor we have asked you." With those words the anjo disappeared into the heavens.

When the middle of the second month came around, Maruya anticipated the moment with great eagerness. She waited, keeping herself pure. Then one evening the Lord came down from heaven in the form of a butterfly and lighted on the face of the Biruzen Maruya. At that moment he named her Santa Maruya of Korodo and flew into her mouth. Immediately she conceived.[40]

When four months had passed, Maruya grew increasingly heavy with child. She thought to herself, "Izaberuna is also with child now and in her last month. She must be having difficulties," and so Maruya set out for Izaberuna's home. At the same moment, Izaberuna was also considering the state of Maruya and said to herself, "Her difficulties are surely greater than mine." So she too started out in the direction of Maruya's home. Because the two women had taken the same road, they met each other at the spot where the Abe River flows.

Izaberuna, greatly surprised when she saw her friend, leaped backwards and then bowed with her head to the ground, and uttered the words: "Maruya, full of grace, to you I bow. The Lord is with you and blessed are you among all other women. Precious is the Jisūsu who is in your womb." Maruya listened and said, "Our Father who is in heaven, hallowed is your name. He will come and may your will be done on earth as it is in heaven. From heaven give us our daily nourishment."[41]

From Maruya's womb the child heard the words both women had spoken to each other. That is why after his birth the Lord made their words into two prayers: the Hail Mary and the Our Father.

Because these prayers were both composed at the Abe River, they are called the Abe Maruya as a single unit of prayer.[42]

At that time by the river, the two women, Maruya and Izaberuna, had a lot of stories to tell each other. Afterward, they returned by separate roads each to her own home.

❊ ❊ ❊ ❊ ❊ ❊ ❊ ❊ ❊ ❊ ❊ ❊ ❊ ❊ ❊ ❊

5. The Tribulations of Santa Maruya

WHEN SANTA MARUYA arrived home that day, for the first time her parents detected that their daughter was pregnant. Furious, they spoke harshly, berating her, "You who spurned the king, where and from what kind of person is this child that fills your belly?[43] We can't understand your debauchery. If word of this should reach the king we will all be destroyed. Not another minute will you be allowed to traipse around this house like that." They continued to scold her, trembling with anger all the while. "Get out of here this very minute" were their last words.

Maruya had no choice but to leave her home sobbing. She wandered, and stayed for awhile now here and now there, and lay down in the fields and at the foot of mountains. Under the eaves of strangers' homes she lingered. Nothing can really compare to the difficulties she experienced. At last, in the middle of the eleventh month, she wandered into the country of Beren.[44] Heavy snows had begun to fall there, and thinking how much she would like shelter for just a little while, she entered a stable. There among the cows and horses she crouched down and sheltered herself. In that stable from noon until midnight she observed *zeshin*.[45] Then at midnight she gave birth. This was the birth of the Holy One.

On account of the intense cold in the stable, the Holy One's body was in danger of freezing. But the cows and horses that surrounded the mother and child breathed their warm breath on the newborn. Thanks to them the holy body was warmed and endured the winter cold. In a manger in that stable the newborn also took his first bath.[46]

Because of the great compassion that the horses and cattle showed, we are not allowed to eat meat or poultry on Wednesdays.[47]

As dawn arrived, the stable owner's wife and others came out of the house to see. "Well, just imagine, in a sty like this you had a safe delivery," said the owner's wife. "Come into our house," she urged Maruya, and guided her inside where they took care of Maruya in various ways and treated her kindly.

After three days had passed, Maruya requested a bath. When the bath was over she said to the lady of the house, "Please, let your son bathe in the same water." But the woman answered, "I am grateful for your thoughtfulness, but my son is diseased and his life is hanging by a thread. Excuse my rudeness if I refuse." But Maruya encouraged her, saying, "Please, let him get in." So the boy's mother put her sickly son in the bath and his disease vanished and he was cured instantly. The power of that water had restored his very life.[48]

On the eighth day the Holy One—reflecting on this transient world with its desires, cruelty, and the lingering attachments of the heart—underwent *shirukushisan*.[49] When his blood flowed out, the Holy Mother, Santa Maruya, was extremely shocked and cried while she clung to him.

Not much time had passed since the Holy One's birth when Menteo the King of Turkey, Gasuparu the King of Mexico, and Bautozaru the King of France each separately had received an oracle and set out on their journey.[50] Although the roads they took were separate, mysteriously, the three roads converged at a certain point and the three kings happened to meet there. From that moment on they traveled as a group. As a guide they had a shining star so that they arrived presently in Beren.

Now the King of Beren at that time was Yorotetsu,[51] and when the three kings reached him they said, "We have each received an oracle that in this country the Lord of Heaven will soon be born. This is what brings us to your kingdom. Please tell us where the Lord of Heaven may be found."

Yorotetsu listened and answered, "Well, this is the first I've heard of it." The kings pressed Yorotetsu saying, "Yorotetsu, you should come with us also to worship him." But Yorotetsu snapped back, "No, I won't go. Why don't you go first?"

"We will," said the three kings and departed from the presence of Yorotetsu. But looking at the sky, how cruel it seemed, for the guiding star had vanished. The three kings folded their hands in prayer and turned their faces toward the heavens. Full of remorse, they thought, "What a pity. This probably happened because we visited that evil place." Then they begged: "In some way, please, let us see your light again." The guiding star suddenly appeared and, in fact, it seemed close enough that you could hold it in your hands. They pressed on then, thinking, "Now we are free to continue our journey." Presently, they arrived at the spot they had long sought, and worshiped there. It was the thirteenth day after the Holy One's birth.

When the Lord saw the three kings he asked, "Where did you three come from?" The kings answered him saying, "We are all witnesses of the Star of Proof of the Lord. We each came here led by intuition." The Lord answered them, "The road which you just took to get here is the road of sinful men. That is why it will now disappear. But I will make three roads so that you may return to your countries." While the three kings bowed to the ground and waited with bated breath, in a moment a bridge with three different paths hung suspended from heaven.[52] Each king took his own road, and returned unimpeded and safely to his own country.

The sovereign of Beren, King Yorotetsu, called his two chief retainers Ponsha and Piroto to his side.[53] "I have heard that the Lord of Heaven is to be born in our country," he said. "If we leave things as they are, sooner or later our country will be overrun and captured by him. From me right down to you, my subjects, we will all become strangers and wanderers in our own land. How would you like *that*?"

Then Ponsha and Piroto asked, "What kind of person is this Lord of Heaven?" The king answered, "Well, he's just a babe now. No more than fourteen or fifteen nights have passed since his birth." Hearing this, the two retainers scoffed, "There's no need to fear that bratty child. We'll just go and pluck him between our fingers and squeeze the life out of him. So set your heart at ease, King."

The retainers Ponsha and Piroto made haste and departed for they knew not where. They wandered through fields and mountains, crossed a river, and went from town to town and house to house. They left not a single house they passed unsearched. They looked everywhere.

The Holy One and Santa Maruya, who had learned of the search, had already fled together. What else could they do? And as they were wandering, not knowing where to go, they came across a group of people in a field sowing wheat. They turned to these sowers, saying, "We have a favor to ask of you. We are being hunted down. If our pursuers should come and ask after us, please do us the favor of saying, 'In the season when we were sowing they passed this way.'"

But the wheat sowers only laughed at them, saying, "We are sowing now, so if we were to say 'in the season when we were sowing,' indeed it would be an odd thing to say, wouldn't it?" It is said that the wheat these sowers planted never grew.

Maruya and the Holy One continued in their flight. Once again they came across wheat sowers in a field and asked as before. But this time the sowers replied to their request, "Of course, we will tell your pursuers just as you have asked us." The Lord was happy that these wheat sowers had agreed, and as he fled with his mother he thought, "Wheat, ripen soon!"

The pursuers came running to that field and when they spotted the sowers they yelled down to them, "Hey, you people over there sowing wheat, did two fugitives pass by here?" The wheat sowers listened and said, "Of course, in the season when we were sowing the wheat they passed through." But when the retainers Ponsha and Piroto looked at the wheat, its color had already turned and it was ripe.[54] Hearing this and looking at the wheat, the two felt as if the wind had suddenly been punched out of their sails. They turned back at that field and went home.

The two refugees, Maruya and the Holy One, who had just barely escaped from that danger, arrived at the big river called Bauchisumo. They met San Jiwan there and asked, "Where are you going?" San Jiwan answered, "In order to pour water over you, Lord, I was born seven months earlier." Rejoicing, the Lord urged him on, "Well, then, baptize me in this river." When it was done the Lord was revered as Jusukiri. Indeed, what limpid and miraculous waters these were.

Then the Lord thought, for the salvation of wicked people in the world to come, "Waters, divide!" And as he thought this, so it happened that the waters divided into more than forty thousand rivers. All people who receive of these waters at the end of the rivers would each and every one taste the pleasures of Paraiso.[55]

When the fortieth day came, the Holy One arrived at a place called Taboro. But Deusu thought, "I want to summon the Holy One who is now on earth to come to me," so the Holy One went up to heaven soon after. He talked face-to-face with Deusu who said to him, "I'll give you a rank," and handed him a crown reserved for the Holy One who received it on his head and descended from heaven to Taboro once again.[56]

In Taboro he was ordained and entered the small sanctuary in the forest of Zeze-Maruya.[57] It was then already the fiftieth day, and he began his studies there under the guidance of one called Sagaramento who had descended from heaven in order to instruct him for seven days and nights. After the Holy One had demonstrated his proficiency to Sagaramento's satisfaction, Sagaramento returned to heaven again. The Holy One pursued his studies until he was twelve.[58]

* * * * * * * * * * * * * * * * *
6. The Five Mysteries of the Morning[59]

DURING THE HOLY ONE's twelve years of study his sacred mother, Santa Maruya, gathered spiderwebs wherever she could and wove the webs into heavenly silks. In this way she made many garments for the Holy One.

A nearby place—Barandō—was famous for a person named Gakujūran.[60] When the Holy One heard how Gakujūran was reputed to have mastered the Buddhist scriptures and other texts, he thought, "I want to study with him, too," and he hurried off to Barandō.

For three days and three nights the Holy Mother, Santa Maruya, searched for her son. When at last she found him in Barandō, she rejoiced.

This is the origin of the joyful *orassho* of the mysteries of the morning.

In Barandō, Gakujūran got onto his chair and spoke. "When people say the sacred six-lettered name, 'Namu-Amida-Butsu,'[61] without any doubt they will attain Buddhahood and be reborn in Gokuraku."

The Holy One, who was listening, responded, "If people utter that name, what kind of place will they go to when they die?" Gakujūran answered, "After death, although it will be completely dark, as soon as the deceased boards the Boat of Vows,[62] the wicked will fall into Jikoku while the good will certainly go to Gokuraku."[63]

Again the Holy One asked, "This Gokuraku, where is it?" Gakujūran, ready with an answer, said, "As soon as you board the

Boat of Vows without a doubt you will reach Gokuraku." But the Holy One said, "When you merely say 'without a doubt' I can't really grasp your meaning. I want to ask you how heaven and earth, the sun and moon, humans, and all of creation came into being."

"For a youngster," Gakujūran said, "you certainly talk a lot. Do you really know about such things yourself?" The Holy One listened and said, "I know well and will tell you too." Then Gaku-jūran got off his chair and summoned the Holy One to take it.

The Holy One thus gave his sermon: "From the depth of the earth to the height of heaven measures more than 80,000 *jō*.[64] As for the one you worship as Buddha, he is called Deusu, Lord of Heaven. He is the Buddha who introduced the salvation to help humankind in the world yet to come.

"This Buddha made heaven and earth, the sun and the moon, the heaven called Paraiso, the human creation, and everything else that exists. Indeed, there is nothing that this Buddha cannot make. What's more, at the time he made man he blew in his own breath and created humankind. But later people sighed so much that these sighs became an evil wind and these winds gathered together on the island into a typhoon that wrought destruction. Trees and plants were blown down and the human seed was near to extinction. But from heaven Buddha stopped it, although its destruction had already covered an expanse of 75 *ri*.[65]

Through all this Gakujūran's disciples listened and then pleaded with the Holy One. "It was in order to understand the workings of cause and effect that we chose Gakujūran as our master. But from now on please make us your disciples." The Holy One granted their desire, saying, "Your wish has conquered me." He then took water and poured it over the twelve, baptizing them. They made a mutual promise—that of master and disciple. What's more, after that time whenever they visited the temple, mobs of people came and begged them saying, "Me too! Me too! I want to be baptized." So there at Barandō the twelve served as Konesoru.[66]

Witnessing all of this, Gakujūran thought, "I should also respect him as my master and become his disciple." The Holy One told Gakujūran that his books were all useless and ought to be thrown out. But Gakujūran objected and said such things as, "These are the *Issai-kyō*,[67] and important sutras." This kind of argument had no end, so the Holy One said, "All right, if you say so, but let us inquire into the truth of the matter with a simple test. We will measure the weight of this one book against your many books." They set them on the scales, and the many books were light but the one book was much heavier.

Seeing this proof, Gakujūran could argue no longer and also desired to receive the waters and be baptized. After this Gakujūran said, "Yorotetsu is now searching for you in earnest. Leave this temple just as it is and let these books stay just where they are, and baptize me now." So the Holy One baptized Gakujūran and set off for Roma together with his twelve disciples.

When they had arrived in the country called Roma, they built a glittering temple there. It was studded with silver and gold. This was the temple of Santa Ekirenja.[68] Here at this temple they spread their teaching of salvation concerning the world to come.

❖ ❖ ❖ ❖ ❖ ❖ ❖ ❖ ❖ ❖ ❖ ❖ ❖ ❖ ❖ ❖ ❖

7. A Nationwide Search

ALTHOUGH KING YOROTETSU searched feverishly for the Holy One, soaring high and digging into the deepest crevices, he was unable to find the hiding place in the whole Kingdom of Beren. He felt anxious and feared that the Holy One might be lost among the masses of common people. For this reason he commanded that all children in his land from newborns up to those seven years of age be killed with no exceptions. The number of infanticides reached a total of 44,444.[69] Each one of them was executed, and if you say that this was a sacrilege and a pity, that is simply not sufficient. For there are really no words that can express the cruelty of this deed.

When word of this heinous act reached the Holy One's ears he thought, "Thousands of children have lost their lives on my account." This is why for the sake of the salvation of the world to come he withdrew into the forest of Zeze-Maruya and performed all kinds of austerities.

In this forest the Holy One received an oracle from Deusu: THOUSANDS OF INFANTS LOST THEIR LIVES ON YOUR ACCOUNT. I FEAR THEY MAY NOW FORFEIT THE PLEASURE OF PARAISO. FOR THEIR SAKE IN THE NEXT WORLD, YOU MUST BE TORTURED AND TRODDEN UPON. SUFFER AND GIVE UP YOUR BODY. The Holy One then fell suddenly to the ground, and beads of sweat and blood poured down from him.

This is the origin of the *orassho* of the five mysteries of the day.[70]

After his retreat in the forest, the Holy One returned to the temple of Santa Ekirenja in Roma, thinking, "In some way I want to lose my life tormented by wicked men."

Now among his disciples one was called Judatsu. An evil idea suddenly possessed him and wheedled its way inside him where it lodged deep and snug. He thought that because the Holy One, his master, was being hunted at that very moment, if he betrayed him by telling Yorotetsu of Beren where the Holy One was, then he himself would receive a handsome reward.

The Holy One, who could discern the innermost thoughts of people, came to realize the situation. He announced to his disciples, "Among my twelve disciples one of you is my enemy." Having heard this they responded in unison, "Not one of us is harboring that sort of hidden plan." But the Holy One insisted, "The person who eats his rice with soup every morning is the one who will betray me."[71]

Eventually Judatsu's evil wish grew stronger, and one Wednesday morning after he had finished eating early as usual, he hurried off to Beren. Soon after he met with King Yorotetsu and told him, "King, for some time now you have been searching for the Lord. Well, he is the chief priest in the temple of Santa Ekirenja in Roma. Arrest him as soon as possible and execute him."

Yorotetsu listened, and was extremely pleased by the information. He gave Judatsu a great deal of money saying, "You can have as big a reward as you desire."

Judatsu, carrying his money reward, was returning along the road to Santa Ekirenja when all of a sudden he was transformed. His nose grew huge and his tongue long. He wondered then what he could do about it, but as there seemed to be no ready solution, he went back to Santa Ekirenja sobbing.

The other disciples had gathered together and one after the other admonished him, saying, "Now look here, Judatsu, you must have betrayed our master. You treacherous bastard. That's why you look the wretched way you do." Judatsu, ashamed, threw the money away beside the temple, ran away to a thicket in the forest, and hanged himself.[72]

That is the origin of the money mound beside the temple of Ekirenja.[73]

✳ ✳ ✳ ✳ ✳ ✳ ✳ ✳ ✳ ✳ ✳ ✳ ✳ ✳ ✳ ✳ ✳

8. Yorotetsu Captures the Holy One

YOROTETSU IN BEREN was rounding up his forces in order to capture the Holy One. He organized Ponsha and Piroto and an army of people. He hurried them off to Roma. When they arrived at the temple of Santa Ekirenja, they surrounded it in two columns and Ponsha and Piroto shouted out the command, "Don't let him escape." But the Holy One, unruffled, only asked, "Where has Judatsu gone?" The disciples answered, "We upbraided him for his hideous appearance, and so ashamed was he that he ran to the mountains and there he took his own life."

The Holy One listened and said, "As it was preordained that I suffer and give up my life tortured, how I regret Judatsu's end. Even though he betrayed me, I would have helped him if he had not killed himself first."

From the mountains the fire of Naraku and the flames of Inuheruno rose up from the belly of the earth;[74] they burned their way upward. This was a sign for the wicked captors to see, and it did alarm them greatly. Nevertheless, they fastened a rope around the Holy One's neck and bound his arms behind his back.

What a sacrilege, the way the Holy One was dragged to Beren! It was no different than prodding a lamb the way they fastened the cord around his neck and beat him from behind saying, "Get moving! Faster!" Then they beat him with a stick saying, "You dullard," and against his will they pulled him along all the way to Beren.

When at last he was set before King Yorotetsu, the king looked at the captors and said, "Well, well, well. I do appreciate the trouble you've taken." He then added, "I hear that this person called the Lord performs miracles. In that case, don't take your eyes off him, and tie him to this stone pillar."

"Certainly," the captors responded, and tied him as they had been told to do. Then they beat him hard enough to break his bones, and the very bamboo pole they were using split.[75]

Into the Holy One's mouth they placed bitter and spicy things, and rammed them down his throat. Then they dropped a metal crown on his head, and sweat and blood flowed down his body like water from a cascade.[76] Yorotetsu said in anger, "All because of *that* person I went and murdered thousands of children. Make a structure with a length of thirty-three and have him drag it up Karuwaryu Hill.[77] Then crucify him there." Again they took the Holy One against his will.

※※※※※※※※※※※※※※※※

9. Up Karuwaryu Hill

IN A PLACE called Sanchiishima,[78] an enormous tree called the Cross Tree grows.[79] Its height is sixty-six units of 6 *shaku*, and the girth of its trunk is thirty-three units of 6 *shaku*. The trunk portion is reserved for future use. The tree will ultimately be set on fire by Deusu, who will descend from heaven for this express purpose. This fire will have no end and will continue to burn. The fire will travel through all of its veins and branches, and when the tree is completely burned up so too will the whole world. Fire from heaven and fire from earth will join each other within a span of six hours. How terrible and dreadful it will be!

Thus the upper thirty-three units of 6 *shaku* were cut from the Cross Tree and made into a crucifixion rack. The captors then attached the cross to the Holy One's shoulders and pushed him up Karuwaryu Hill.

On the way up the hill the Holy One met a woman named Beronica who was carrying a jug of water.[80] She felt compassion when she saw him. "How pitiful," she thought, and wiped the beads of blood dripping from his face with her cloth, and offered him a drink of water. The Holy One received it with gratitude and drank, thinking, "I don't know who you are but one day I will save you." Then because the image of the Holy One remained on Beronica's cloth she thought, "Keeping this for myself would be a sacrilege." So she made an offering of the cloth at the temple of Santa Ekirenja.

After a little more time had passed, the Lord was forced to continue upward until he reached the top of Karuwaryu Hill. There were two criminals condemned to death up there. The Lord was placed between those two and his hands and feet nailed with big nails. On both sides the other two were bound and raised. The criminal on the left said, "There are many ways of being executed, but a crueler way than this has never been devised. This is all because of you, Lord," he complained.

The criminal on the right side hearing this said, "You're totally wrong. We're guilty convicts. The Holy One has committed no crime and so his execution is truly pitiful."

Now there is some background to these criminals. After the Lord's birth and the taking of his first bath, the diseased child bathed in the same water. Although he was nearly dead from disease, after bathing in that water he recovered miraculously in an instant. Nevertheless, when he grew up he became a wicked person, and in the end wound up a condemned criminal.[81] Yet now he was together again with the Lord for his last moments on a cross. It was his fate that they should meet again.

✼ ✼ ✼ ✼ ✼ ✼ ✼ ✼ ✼ ✼ ✼ ✼ ✼ ✼ ✼ ✼ ✼ ✼

10. Money Bedazzled

DAY AFTER DAY in monotonous succession, tortures on Karuwaryu Hill continued. Hearing of this turn of events and lamenting, the forty-six disciples performed various austerities: fasting, laughing in death's face, they held firm to the desire to imitate the Holy One's way.[82] The Holy One too discerned that they were performing all of these austerities and composed the Go-passho Orassho.[83]

Impatient, Yorotetsu said repeatedly, "Soldiers, hurry up and snuff out his spirit at its very source." Making obeisances, they took up their swords, but no matter how hard they tried, their bodies lost their strength; their arms and legs would not even move, so that they were unable to pierce the Holy One.

Then a blind man came along, and they said to him, "See here, blind man. In this place someone is nailed to a cross. If you deal him the death blow we'll give you some money. How about it, eh?" The blind man listened and said, "If you will just show me where, I'll jab him." So the samurai guard said, "Over here, this is it," and guided him carefully. "Oh, I see," said the blind man and with an "ummph," he jabbed his spear into the Holy One.

Blood spurted out and poured down over the blind man. When it ran into his eyes, in an instant both eyes were miraculously opened. "How extraordinary indeed," he marveled, saying, "This world has become bright. If only I had stabbed that wicked person sooner, these eyes too would have been opened earlier."

This time the Holy One said, "Blind man, you shall not be saved in the world to come." After the blind man had given the Holy One the death blow without any qualms and received his money reward, his vision was suddenly extinguished, and he returned to his former state of blindness.

This is the origin of our saying, "Eyes darkened by money."[84]

Together with the criminals on his left and right, the three vanished transient as smoke. But the criminal on the right with gratitude accompanied the Holy One up to heaven. What a sad sight, though, as the one on the left sank into Inuheruno all by himself.

It was natural that the mother Santa Maruya wailed and raved when she saw the corpse of the Holy One. King Yorotetsu, looking on, asked a soldier, "Over there a maiden is sobbing. Who is she?" The soldier reported back, "She is the mother of the Holy One who was crucified." King Yorotetsu listened and said, "Then it's only the natural grief of a parent and child being separated. Permit her to stay with him."

The Holy Mother threw herself down, clinging to the corpse.[85] She wept so bitterly that the guards thought, "Her tears have no end." They then took the dead body and put it in a stone coffin, and lowered it in the ground. From then on a guard kept watch over the spot day and night.[86]

✻ ✻ ✻ ✻ ✻ ✻ ✻ ✻ ✻ ✻ ✻ ✻ ✻ ✻ ✻ ✻ ✻

11. The Kirinto[87]

ON FRIDAY the Holy One came down to earth and remained there until Saturday. He stood on top of his coffin and many of his disciples came to worship him. He then returned to heaven and on the third day he sat on the right side of Deusu, his Parent. After that, for the sake of the salvation of both the living and the dead, he descended from heaven and went to the temple of Santa Ekirenja.

This is the origin of the five mysteries of the evening.[88]

His head disciple—Pappa—went to see the Holy One at the Gate of Virtue. There the Holy One remained for forty days and taught him all about salvation and the afterlife. He gave sermons to his Abosutoro for ten days, and on the fiftieth day he returned to heaven.[89]

The Holy Mother Maruya then received an oracle from heaven, and on the third of the seventh month she ascended to heaven from Mount Oribete.[90] In heaven, however, the Holy Mother is the Mediator, and the Holy One is the Savior. Deusu is the Father or Paateru, the Holy One is the Son or Hiiriyo, and the Holy Mother is the Suheruto Santo. Deusu became three bodies although they were originally One.[91]

✳ ✳ ✳ ✳ ✳ ✳ ✳ ✳ ✳ ✳ ✳ ✳ ✳ ✳ ✳ ✳ ✳ ✳ ✳

12. The Holy One's Selection

THE THOUSANDS of children who Yorotetsu had massacred years before had been wandering ever since in Koroteru. The Holy One gave them all names and brought them to Paraiso.[92] Then he chose the owner of the inn where he was born, followed by the Three Kings of Turkey, Mexico, and France. He did not omit a single disciple, nor the second group of wheat sowers, and Beronica the woman who gave him water. He brought them all as a group to Paraiso.

The Holy Mother Maruya then turned to Deusu and said, "Someone died of love for me because of my religious austerities and my vow to remain a *biruzen*." Then she implored Deusu, "Please save the person I am referring to, and raise him to the rank of my husband."

Thus Deusu saved the King of Roson and made Maruya and the king man and wife. He gave the king the rank called Zejūsu, related to that of the Holy One. Beronica who carried water received the rank of Aneisuteru, the protector of charitable works in this world.[93]

✳ ✳ ✳ ✳ ✳ ✳ ✳ ✳ ✳ ✳ ✳ ✳ ✳ ✳ ✳ ✳ ✳ ✳ ✳

13. Establishment of the Officials

SAN MIGIRI received the position of keeping the scales.[94] In the temple of Jurisharen,[95] he inquires about the sins and lets the good people go to Paraiso and the bad people fall to Inheruno. Depending also on the circumstances of the sins, he punishes them in such a way that sinful people feel ashamed of their sins.

Even though a person is good, the *tengu* will still try to possess him. But Migiri with his almighty knife scatters them. He does not want to give a person up to the *tengu*, so he lets them go instead to Furukatoriya.[96] Those who make a complete confession he frees from the clutches of Inuheruno.

But those who have committed suicide or have harmed others, they will undergo investigation but in any case will still be thrown into Inuheruno. They will never be saved, so you must be careful.[97]

San Peitoro is the gate official. When you reach the gate you must offer the Gate-Opening Orassho.[98] San Pauro evaluates the good and the evil, and those who are neither good nor evil will go to Furukatoriya; it all depends on the nature of their sins. They may undergo examination anywhere from six hours to thirty-three years.[99] Afterward, San Jiwan will inspect, Abosutoro will forgive, and through Santosu the Mediator they will soon experience the pleasures of Paraiso.[100]

✳ ✳ ✳ ✳ ✳ ✳ ✳ ✳ ✳ ✳ ✳ ✳ ✳ ✳ ✳ ✳ ✳

14. The Destruction of Our World

WHEN THE TIME draws near for the destruction of this world, a great fireball will descend. Winds will roar, torrential rains fall, and insects plague the earth. All kinds of human negligence will be visible. For seven years things will remain in this chaotic state. That is why food shortages will be rampant and the food and possessions of affluent people will be taken from them by force. When their food is all eaten up, people will start turning on their neighbors and nearly devour one another.[101]

The *tengu* will arrive at this time. With a secret desire to entice people into their power they will transform the fruit of the *masan* into various alluring shapes and appealing objects, and offer it to people in many guises. Those who eat of this fruit will fall into the *tengu*'s hands and drop into Inuheruno.[102]

After another seven years have elapsed, in the subsequent three years rice paddies and fields as far as the mountains and in all directions will bear rich harvests. It will be an age of luxury, ease, and extraordinary abundance. This is the last chance for people to give up their evil ways and begin to practice virtue. Then you will have salvation.

When another three years have elapsed, the fire from the sun and the fire from below the earth will join, and the Cross Tree of Sanchiishima will burn up completely. Seawater will turn to oil and the fire will blaze high. Grasses and trees too will burn like candlewicks. In twelve places the blazes will burn and rise to dreadful heights. When beasts, birds, and other living things see this, they will cry out, "Oh, help us! We want to be saved, so let us be eaten by humans and have a chance."[103]

The blazing fires will rise gradually and within three units of time die out. After this great conflagration, as far as the eye can see, this world will be a vast expanse of white sand. Santosu will blow his shell trumpet, and the humans who were made first, then those who died long long ago, and finally those who died consumed in the recent conflagration will appear in the vast clearing. Every one of them without exception will show up in that place. Thus Deusu whose power is infinite will make souls appear again with their original bodies.[104]

It is said that at that time some souls will be wandering about. When we look into the reason for this situation, the answer lies in practices of our present world. For the wandering souls are those of people who were cremated.[105] They are destined to roam about for all eternity. They can never float up to the light but must remain in perpetual darkness.

But at the time of this great holocaust, bodies buried in the ground or thrown in the water, eaten up by beasts, birds, or fish, will all return to their original forms despite their various ways of dying.[106] But it is a different matter for a human body that has been eaten by another human. Those will never again return to their original forms.

This is the reason we do not take medicines made from mummies.[107]

Deusu the Almighty will descend from heaven and blaze a trail through the myriad souls. Within three units of time Deusu will select some and mark them with his seal. All of them will be divided either on Deusu's left or Deusu's right. What a sad thing to see those on the left who, because they did not receive baptism, will fall together with the *tengu* to the hell called Benbō and get their stamp there. For all of eternity they will never float up to the light from the depths to where they have sunk.

Those people on the right who received baptism will accompany Deusu to Paraiso where, once judged, their good works will be the basis of the ranks they will receive. It is guaranteed that they will all become buddhas[108] and know unlimited fulfillment for eternity. Ammei Zesusu.[109]

❀ ❀ ❀ ❀ ❀ ❀ ❀ ❀ ❀ ❀ ❀ ❀ ❀ ❀ ❀ ❀

15. Addendum

ONCE THERE WERE two friends. The world had never seen the likes of them for closeness. One of them said to the other, "If you die before I do, please tell me in full detail what the hereafter is like. But if I die first, I'll report to you within three days." They made a pact to this effect. However, when one of them died, the remaining one grieved terribly, tumbling to the ground and crying to heaven. Although he grieved and cried, it was of no use, for already three days and nights had passed with still no news from his friend.

Three years also passed, and because he received not a word from his friend, he gave up his pleading together with his hope, and had nearly died from all his yearning. Then three years later, in the third month, his deceased friend returned, and the living one rejoiced beyond measure and asked, "Why did you take so long?" His friend answered, "I didn't have a moment to spare."

Looking at him, his appearance was changed from its previous state. Under his jaw specks of fire could be seen burning. So his friend asked, "How did that fire get there?" "Oh, this is the fire of Furukatoriya," his friend replied.

After hearing this the living friend said, "In that case, give the fire to me. I will destroy my sins now while in this world. Then let's leave the world behind together." "Forget it," said his friend. "The heat of this fire is ten times that of the fire in this world. It's extremely difficult to endure." But the living one said, "I don't care a single bit—give it to me." So his friend answered, "If that's what you really want, it's all yours."

They heaped up all the trees that were growing nearby and lit them with the fire of Meido.[110] The burning flames rose incessantly and in an instant the body had burned up. Soon after, he gained the way to heaven and joined the multitude in Paraiso. He is the one whom we call Santosu-sama,[111] but because we do not know the name of the other friend we have omitted it.

✳ ✳ ✳ ✳ ✳ ✳ ✳ ✳ ✳ ✳ ✳ ✳ ✳ ✳ ✳ ✳ ✳
Notes

Introduction

1. This edict did not condemn only the Christian religion. It was equally harsh in its condemnation of the Buddhist sect Fuju-Fuse, whose principle, "not receiving from and not giving to non-believers," was advocated by its founder, Nichio (1565–1630) of the Nichiren sect. The edict was, in fact, directed at all those who "do nothing for the temple." Both Fuju-Fuse and Christianity would have qualified as adamant nonsupporters. From the issuance of this edict, Buddhist priests were assigned the role of inquisitors in the service of the state. They were compelled to visit the homes of all their parishioners at Obon (the Buddhist "All Soul's Day") to read the sutras and examine the family altars for any signs of heretical worship. For an English translation of the edict see Gubbins (1877–1878).

2. The original *fumi-e* were images that officials confiscated from Christian family altars. In the catechism, *Doctrina Christan,* Christians were urged to place numerous sacred images on and surrounding their altars. The early *fumi-e* were paper pictures, but because they wore out easily, the government officials began to make cast brass images embedded in wood. Trampling on the image was considered sufficient evidence of not being a Christian. Indeed, at the outset of the practice, Dutch traders too were subjected to the *e-fumi* (rite of trampling), and many found it so dis-

tasteful that they refused to return to Japan. When the practice began to threaten trade relations with the Dutch, the shogun abandoned it among the Dutch. Jonathan Swift made this rite famous in *Gulliver's Travels*, Part 3, Chapter 11 (Kataoka 1981:35, 159).

3. In 1601, the first Japanese Jesuit priests—Sebastião Kimura, S.J., and Luis Niabara, S.J.—were ordained. But by the time of the generalized persecutions beginning in 1614, there were only seven Japanese Jesuit priests (Schütte 1975:579–587). Of the other three orders, during the entire "Christian Century" the Franciscans produced only one Japanese priest and the Dominicans and the Augustinians could count only three and two respectively (Cieslik 1981: 12–13).

4. The statistics vary on this point. To list but a few, Gonoi places the figure at 760,000 (1990:12), although he has not subtracted apostates and martyrs. Schütte lists as many as 500,000 for 1614 (1968:433). Kataoka estimates between 450,000 and 600,000 (1974:17). Boxer estimates 300,000 (1951:321). I have decided to follow the reasoning of Elison, who chooses 300,000 as a rough estimate (1988:397).

5. Father Petitjean's original letters are kept in the archives of the Missions-Etrangères de Paris headquarters in Paris in several volumes (personal communication with the director of the MEP Archives, Fr. Gerard Moussay, 13 July 1995).

6. This figure also varies from 40,000 to 60,000. Cary lists 50,000 (1976:288); Cooper lists 60,000 (1983:308). My figure is based on a table found in *Missions-Etrangères, Comptes Rendus* of 1878. It lists 17,380 Catholics and 30,000 schismatics, "Kakure Kirishitan," or roughly 50,000 in all.

7. Three well-documented pictures that portray the rosary survived the persecutions. Two of these are of Jesuit origin, as they also depict the Jesuit saints Francis Xavier and Ignatius Loyola. The third one from Urakami, destroyed in 1945, was probably Franciscan. (For reproductions see Cooper 1971:135–136, 155.)

8. Although scholars have various definitions for these ancient Christians, *sempuku kirishitan* (Secret Christians) generally refers to those who hid out of necessity. *Kakure kirishitan* (Hidden Chris-

tians) refers to those who continued to hide long after necessity dictated this position. *Hanare kirishitan* (Separate Christians) was a term the Meiji-era missionaries used in reference to those ancient Christians who refused to be reconciled with the Catholic church. *Korobi kirishitan* (Fallen Christians), a much older term, was used in reference to those *kirishitan* who apostasized under the pressure of torture. Today these ancient Christians refer to themselves simply as Kakure (The Hidden).

9. After the fall of the Tokugawa shogunate and the establishment of the new Meiji government in 1868, the ban on Christianity was renewed by the new Meiji government. From the years 1869 to 1873, Christians in Kyushu and the Gotō Islands suffered persecution. As many as four thousand were exiled to remote parts of Japan, and others were put in overcrowded jails. Owing somewhat to foreign pressure, the anti-Christian signboards were eventually removed and Christians were able to practice their religion without grave harassment. The Meiji Constitution (1889) was the first legal guarantee of religious freedom, although this freedom was conditional. For detailed information on the Christian exiles see Urakawa Wasaburō's *Kirishitan no Fukkatsu* (1979: vol. 2) and *Gotō Kirishitan-shi* (1973:101–226).

10. José García Delgado, O.P., a Spanish Dominican and longterm resident in Shikoku, is an authority on the Christian history of Japan. He suspects present-day Kakure Kirishitan activity on the Koshikijima archipelago, located off the coast of Kagoshima. A local shrine in Katanoura is referred to locally as "Ebisu-Deusu," and the ringing style of the Buddhist temple bell is Castilian. Delgado's visit appears to have been too brief to confirm or negate his supposition (Delgado 1985a:68).

11. I was taught about these two styles directly from *mizukata* Iwamura Yoshinobu (b. 1900) of Narushima. The arrangement of dishes on the two offering trays differs according to the two styles. Both styles arrange four bowls and one flat plate on each tray. The bowls contain sake on one tray and cooked rice on the other. The flat dish holds fish. In the *kamikata* style, the plate of fish is placed in the upper right corner of the tray. In the *shimokata* style, the

plate of fish is placed in the lower right corner of the tray. In addition, the *kamikata* is considered the stricter of the two styles owing to the fact that the Kakure Kirishitan perform their service a day in advance of the actual feast day. Iwamura did not know the origin of these two styles. Their meaning has also consistently eluded researchers of the Kakure Kirishitan (Ōno 1989:134–135; Furuno 1984:231–235).

12. Precise statistics on the number of Kakure Kirishitan are difficult to obtain. Tagita estimates 30,000 (1965:1:141), a figure which matches that found in the table of the *Missions-Etrangères, Comptes Rendus* for the year 1878. It seems an inflated estimate, and in any case the figure would depend on how one defines Kakure Kirishitan. Who should be counted: those who are actual practitioners of the religion or those whose background is Kakure Kirishitan and thus are socially defined as such regardless of their actual religious affiliation? The island of Narushima has a population of 4,893 (Naru-chō Kikakuzai-seika 1993: Data 3), and the total number of villages, including offshore Maeshima, is twenty-two. Of these, fourteen are Kakure Kirishitan, one is predominantly Catholic, and the remaining are Shinto and Buddhist. Thus 70 percent of the islanders have Kakure Kirishitan origins—although only seven active officials are still living and fewer than fifty people practice the religion with any regularity.

13. Many Kakure Kirishitan have returned to Shinto as a religion. Women who were once Kakure Kirishitan now often participate in various shamanistic folk religious circles where the members meet at least once a month. The majority of villagers in the Kakure Kirishitan village of Yagami joined Sōka Gakkai. Some individual Kakure Kirishitan have joined Tenri-kyō, and still others have converted to Catholicism. On Fukeujima, several have joined Ōmoto-kyō.

14. Of the thirty families from Shittsu registered at Tempukuji, twenty of them actively practice both Buddhism and the Kakure Kirishitan religion (telephone interview with Shioya Hidemi, 2 October and 4 October 1994). This same incident has been described in a highly personalized manner elsewhere: "The Kakure

esteem him [Shioya Hidemi] so much that some years ago, when restoration of the temple was necessary, each Kakure family donated 80,000 yen" (Volpe 1992:73). This statement does not identify whether the Kakure Kirishitan are those of Kashiyama or Shittsu. In either case, it omits the important facts that the former group became Buddhist and the latter practice a dual religion. Neither can properly be called "Kakure" without some background explanation.

15. According to Tagita, all nine manuscripts were given to the Tenri Library during the war as the "Tagita Collection" (Tagita 1978:46). The library, however, confirms the possession of only two manuscripts of the *Tenchi* and says it has no such "Tagita Collection." Johannes Laures, S.J., in his *Kirishitan Bunko* (1957: 116), refers to Tagita's three manuscripts of the *Tenchi Hajimari no Koto* from Ikitsuki. This appears to be an error, for the same manuscript Laures refers to as KM, Tagita mentions in *Shōwa jidai no sempuku kirishitan*. There it is the Matsuo Kyūichi manuscript from Kurosaki, and Tagita describes it in detail. The manuscript referred to as SH by Laures is probably the Hatakeda Shuhō manuscript; it is from the Gotō Islands. Tagita, who made many recordings of prayers in Ikitsuki that he later transcribed, says: "The Kakure in Ikitsuki have nothing in writing" (Tagita 1966:2:129–130). An Ikitsuki Kakure Kirishitan specialist, Miyazaki Kentarō, confirms that Ikitsuki has no tradition of the *Tenchi Hajimari* (personal communication, 27 September 1994).

16. Narushima, where I conducted my fieldwork for eleven months, established its first public elementary school in 1874. The first middle school was founded in 1947; the first high school in 1965 (Naru-chō Kyōiku Iinkai 1992:242–248). Most Kakure Kirishitan officials are eighty to ninety years old and therefore grew up at a time when elementary school was the highest level of education available to them. Islanders who wished to attend middle school or high school could have done so at an earlier date, however, by sending their children to neighboring Fukuejima or Nagasaki. But this entailed substantial room and board costs and would therefore have excluded the Kakure Kirishitan at that time.

17. Diego Yūki, S.J., an authority on Kirishitan history, views the *Tenchi* as an eclectic mixture based on a hypothetical *Seisho monogatari* (Bible stories), explanations from the *Doctrina Christan,* lives of the saints, and part of a Christmas play (personal communication, 26 May 1994).

18. A later version of the *Doctrina Christan* (1600) contains a larger section devoted to the fifteen mysteries of the rosary.

19. Kojima Yukie divides the *Tenchi* manuscripts into two branches stemming from a hypothetical manuscript based on a hypothetical oral tale. The original text of branch b is the Zen manuscript, from which the following are derived: Suke-Jii, Shimogawa, Gen'emon, Yota, and Ichidaiki. The original text of branch c is the Michiwaki manuscript, from which the Hatakeda derives (Kojima 1969).

Translation

1. *Tenchi Hajimari no Koto,* the title of the whole work, is applicable in content only to the first chapter (of which it is also the title). This chapter describes the creation of heaven and earth, the story of Adam and Eve, the Fall, and the promise of redemption. The expression is suggestive of Shintoism; the first chapter of the *Kojiki* itself begins: "*Tenchi hajimete . . .* " The description that follows in the *Tenchi,* however, develops along Buddhist lines, employing both Buddhist and corrupted Christian nomenclature.

2. "*Somosomo*" or "In the beginning . . ." is the first word of the narrative. The Catholic priest, Fr. Bernard Petitjean, who discovered the Kakure Kirishitan in 1865 in his newly built Ōura Church in Nagasaki, imitates the structure of the *Tenchi* in his *Seikyō Shogaku Yōri* (A Fundamental Catechism of Christian Doctrine). His first chapter is titled *Tenchi Ningen no Hajimari,* and the first word of the text is "*Deusu.*" This work, and his *Seikyō Nikka* (Christian Daily Lessons), were written with the intention of drawing the Kakure Kirishitan to the church. Petitjean purposely employs the same Latin-Iberian lexicon that the Kakure Kirishitan used in the *Tenchi.* The Kakure Kirishitan in turn had preserved this lexicon from the early Kirishitan works published by the Jesuit

press in Japan, which functioned from 1591 until 1614 when the persecution of Christianity began in earnest. Petitjean's extreme sensitivity to the psychology of the Kakure Kirishitan led him to reject the use of a catechism made by the superior of the mission, Prudence Girard, on the grounds that its style would alienate the Kakure Kirishitan of the Nagasaki area who were then surfacing. Father Girard and Fr. Peter Manicou working in Yokohama, and Petitjean and Laucaigne working in Nagasaki, could be seen as opponents in that long and bitter conflict within the Catholic church known as the Rites Controversy. This dispute concerned missionary strategy: should the church allow for cultural accommodation of the Catholic religion? This problem had begun over whether Chinese words ought to be permitted in the expression of Christian concepts, and whether rituals in veneration of ancestors or Confucius were likewise permissible. Matteo Ricci was in favor of accommodation, whereas the Franciscans and Dominicans were shocked by such compromise of the faith. In the first half of the eighteenth century, papal statements explicitly restricted cultural accommodation and forbade converts to practice rites connected with ancestor veneration.

In Japan at the time of its reopening, the Latin-Iberian words introduced in the sixteenth and seventeenth centuries had been completely acculturated by the Kakure Kirishitan and were a vital part of their perception and recognition of what was Christian. Thus accommodation—in terms of preserving this ancient lexicon and using it as a vehicle of instruction—was deemed extremely important by Petitjean.

3. Here the Kakure Kirishitan refer to their divinity as Deusu (Lat. *Deus*). The concept of hierarchy and the preoccupation with ranking is found throughout the *Tenchi* narrative. The word employed, *sō*, is a Buddhist term. The Buddha is said to have thirty-two *sō*, or extraordinary "bodily marks," that distinguish him from ordinary people. The conceit that Deusu has two hundred ranks and forty-two forms implies that besides possessing the thirty-two *sō* of the Buddha, Deusu has many more in addition. Although the *sō* indicate virtues, they are described in strikingly

graphic terms that bring into sharp focus an iconic image of the Buddha. These bodily marks range from (number 5) webbed skin between the fingers to (15) light emanating from the body to a distance of about 3 meters to (27) a tongue that is thin, soft, wide, and so long that if the Buddha sticks it out it covers his whole face up to the hairline. For a full list of the thirty-two *sō,* see the Daiichiron Sutra (*Sōgō Bukkyō Daijiten* 1987:483).

4. Japanese Buddhist tradition added two heavens, the Sun Heaven and the Moon Heaven, to the eight of Indian Buddhism. In the *Tenchi* only the Sun Heaven is named. The remainder, of varying obscurity, derive from Christian sources. My interpretation here follows that of Ebisawa's commentary. Benbō is "limbo." Manbō, while unclear, is possibly "world" (Port. *mundo*) and was probably added as a phonetic companion to Benbō. Oribeten is probably the Mount of Olives (Port. *oliveto*) of the *Doctrina Christan.* This spot was esteemed as hallowed, since Christ is believed to have ascended from there to heaven. Moreover, according to legend Mary's tomb is located at the foot of this mountain.

For Shidai and Godai, see note 6. Pappa refers to the Pope (Port. *papa*). Oroha may derive from the Portuguese word for crown, *coroa,* a small rosary of ten beads known in English as a "chaplet." Chapter 4 of the *Doctrina Christan* refers to *korowa no orasho koto,* a prayer used in the sixteenth century. Konsutanchi and Hora of the text seem to have suffered corruption. In another version, these two words are connected by the particle *no—Konsutanchinohora.* This word has been interpreted elsewhere as Constantinople.

Koroteru, from the Portuguese *hortelo,* a garden surrounded by a wall, here represents Eden. Paraiso (Port. *Paraiso*) was the word used by Portuguese for the Christian heaven. Gokuraku is the Buddhist term for heaven (Ebisawa 1970b:506). Paraiso appears variously in the text as Paraiso, Baraiso, and Haraiso. In Japanese, two kinds of diacritical marks when added to syllables change their pronunciation to either a voiced *"b"* or a semivoiced *"p"* sound. The first consists of two short strokes called *dakuten* in Japanese; the second is a tiny circle referred to as *handakuten.* In old texts these marks are not used consistently, so that several variants of a word are sometimes found in the same text.

5. Angel (Port. *anjo*). Jusuheru is Lucifer. The seven angels of whom Lucifer is head refers to Tobit 12:15, where the angel Raphael says: "I am Raphael, one of the seven angels who stand in attendance on the Lord and enter his glorious presence."

6. In Buddhism the five elements (godai) are earth, water, fire, wind, and space *(kū)*. These elements are the four physical states of solid, liquid, heat, and gas (shidai). The last element—space—was a Buddhist innovation intended to integrate the four traditional elements. The passage in the *Tenchi* recalls the four elements, but salt and oil are unusual inclusions. Salt is symbolic of purity in Shintoism and its use is widespread in Japanese ritual and daily life: sumo wrestlers toss handfuls of salt in the ring, *misogi* (waterfall purification) practitioners have salt thrown on them prior to their immersion, and the finishing touch after cleaning house in Japan is often to leave a tiny dish of salt in the open air. Salt is especially important for purification after contact with death, considered the ultimate pollution in Shinto. Japanese returning from funerals will sprinkle salt on themselves before entering their own homes. Christianity inherited its symbolic use of salt from the Jewish tradition, where it stood for permanence and wisdom and was always used in animal sacrifices to confirm the permanent relationship between God and his people. Jesus' words perpetuated this tradition: "You are the salt of the earth" (Matthew 5:13). Salt has long been used in the baptism of infants and adults by placing a pinch of it in the mouth of the person being baptized, a practice derived from the Roman use of salt for cleansing and exorcising. Salt has also been used in the ritual blessing of holy water since the sixth century.

Oil is included here for similar reasons. The Catholic church customarily used olive oil mixed with balsam in rituals of healing and exorcism and particularly in anointing the sick and dying (James 5:14). Extreme unction, the anointing of the gravely ill, is one of the seven sacraments of the Catholic church.

7. These are Japanized forms of the Portuguese names for the

days of the week: *Segunda* (Monday), *Terça* (Tuesday), *Quarta* (Wednesday), *Quinta* (Thursday), *Sexta* (Friday), *Sabado* (Saturday). These names are still used today by the Kakure Kirishitan when discussing the events in their liturgical calendar. Leaving the names for the days of the week in Portuguese is one way of setting sacred time apart from mundane time.

8. Domeigosu-no-Adan (Lat. *Dominus:* Lord), "Adam who belongs to the Lord," or simply (Port. *Domingo:* Sunday), "Sunday Adam," meaning "Adam who was made on Sunday." According to Genesis 1:27, God made humans on Sunday.

9. Epithet is the same as above: Domeigosu-no-Ewa, or "Eve who belongs to the Lord."

10. Chikorō . . . Tanhō: the origin of these names is unclear, but Bohner states that Tagita believed the Kirishitan invented unusual names for their amusement since the Christian cosmology appeared very strange to them (Bohner 1938:491).

11. See note 16.

12. The European apple (Port. *maça*) was unknown in Japan at this time. The first instance of the word *ringo,* or apple, in Japanese is found in 659 in the *Shinshū Honzō* (New Botanical Compilation). The apples it describes are the various varieties then known in China. The native Japanese apples (*zumi* and *ezo*) were quite small, and in the Kamakura period people ate them as sweets. By the beginning of the Edo period, cultivation of these apples had spread.

Fabian Fucan, former Jesuit turned apostate, was one of the severest and most articulate critics of Christianity and indeed wrote the first systematic refutation of the Catholic religion. When discussing the narrative of the Fall, he had difficulty knowing how to render the fruit into Japanese. In his *Ha Deusu* (Deus Destroyed) he writes: "But this business of 'Don't you dare eat the *maçan!*' (a fruit somewhat like a persimmon) truly is the height of absurdity!" (Elison 1988:274–275).

13. The use of the *ofukyō-suru* (to take medicine) in reference to eating the apple emphasizes the apple's special nature and the altered state of consciousness that will result from eating the fruit of the forbidden tree.

14. *Nodo ni kakari*—the apple "lodged in his throat"—refers to the origin of the so-called Adam's apple, which does not figure in the Bible but was part of popular tradition in the West where the protuberance in men's throats was superstitiously believed to be a trait inherited from humanity's first ancestor—Adam—and evidence of the piece of the forbidden fruit that stuck in his throat. This notion seems to have appealed to the highly visual Japanese imagination.

15. Irrespective of chronological time (Mary and Jesus are not yet born), Adam and Eve offer the prayer to the Virgin Mary: Salve Regina (Hail Holy Queen). This prayer was included in the *Doctrina Christan* published in Amakusa by the Jesuits in 1592. Even today it is a favorite among the Kakure Kirishitan, who refer to it as "Sarube Jina." For a comparison of the original text with a contemporary Kakure Kirishitan version from Narushima see Whelan (1992:379).

16. The Contrition *orassho* refers to the Latin prayer the Confiteor or the Portuguese Contrição: the Act of Contrition. The Kakure Kirishitan commonly refer to this prayer as "Konchirisan." It takes its place in the *Tenchi* as the first prayer, just as it had in the *Doctrina Christan*. The full Konchirisan, the *Konchirisan no ryaku* (Essentials of Contrition), was published by the Jesuit Press in 1603. It was extremely important to the underground Christians since it explained how they could be forgiven for sins without the mediation of an ordained priest. This was one of the old documents that emerged with the Kakure Kirishitan of Urakami who began to seek out the French priests. Bishop Urakawa claimed that many copies were in circulation among the Kirishitan. In 1869, Bishop Petitjean reprinted it. The work is composed of five parts that include instructions and explanations. Petitjean also includes a copy in his *Seikyō Nikka* (Christian Daily Prayers).

Another name for this prayer is *Zajime*, which refers to a former practice in the Catholic church of reciting an Act of Contrition immediately after kneeling down in the confessional or after taking a seat in the pew before mass (Ebisawa 1970b:507). The Kakure Kirishitan have preserved the tradition: as soon as they sit down on the floor, they too offer a prayer they call *Zajime*. Although the word itself has become synonymous with prayer, the recited prayer may vary. For the complete text known as *Jūshihi ka Jō* (The Seventeen Articles) in Gotō, see Tagita (1978:449–456).

17. According to Christian tradition, Adam's sin was considered less grave than Eve's since it was not Adam but Eve who was deceived (1 Timothy 2:14). This is often offered as justification for the more severe punishment that Eve receives, interpreted here in terms of her transformation into a lower form of life (a dog) and her assignment to a lower heaven (Middle Heaven).

18. "On the earth there is a stone called *gōjaku*": The word used for earth here is *gekai,* a Buddhist term, literally "lower world," which refers to the earth and is also employed in the *Doctrina Christan* with the same meaning. The stone is known in the local dialect as *gōjaku-no-ishi* and in Japanese as *onjaku,* or "warming stone." It is a kind of serpentine or mica schist occurring naturally and in quantity on the Nishi-Sonogi peninsula northwest of Nagasaki where several Kakure Kirishitan communities still live today. In the nearby mountains of Ōseto-machi, the remains of eight small factories for making pots of this stone have been discovered and date from the Kamakura and Heian periods.

This stone was important because of its durability and softness. Easily cut with a simple tool, it also maintained heat for extended periods without breakage. Due to this unique property, it was used for tombstones, paving stones, and stoves; because of its flatness the stone was readily used as a pocket warmer. When broken into a powder, the powder was then heated, wrapped in a cloth, and used as a foot or hand warmer much like the *hokaron* bought in pharmacies and used widely today in Japan (Kudamatsu 1989:30–32). As the Kakure Kirishitan of Gotō emigrated from Sotome in the 1790s, they brought this useful stone with them. The Gotō Islands, of newer geological formation than the Kyushu mainland, did not produce the stone. Its importance is acknowledged in the *Tenchi,* where the presence of the stone and the rightful homeland of the Kakure Kirishitan are joined.

19. Lucifer is here transformed into a monster that is a hybrid

cross between a Western devil and a Japanese *tengu*. *Tengu* was the word the Jesuits chose to translate "devil" or "Satan" in the early Christian literature they printed in Japan; its use is found in Chapter 2 of the *Doctrina Christan*. The missionaries' decision to translate this concept instead of keeping a Portuguese or Latin word had complex implications for the Kakure Kirishitan. In Japan, *tengu* were worshiped by both *yamabushi* and Buddhists, who conducted fire rituals as a means of absorbing the *tengu* power for various kinds of spiritual empowerment. They maintained a deep respect for the trickster-like *tengu,* which was very much alive in popular and folk religion in rural areas.

In the Japanese literary tradition, *tengu* are demons who inhabit woods and mountains where they often represent the enemies of Buddhism and are known for their protean power to assume various shapes in order to delude people, especially those in the religious professions. In the Japanese Christian tradition, the *tengu* retained their ancient role as the enemy of religion and religious people, but the religion in this case shifted from Buddhism to Christianity.

20. At the opening of the narrative Jusuheru has thirty-two forms, but after committing his grave sin he is demoted to only ten forms. From Ten (Heaven), Deusu assigns him to Chūten (Middle Heaven), the same heaven to which Ewa was relegated in her transformation into a dog. Middle Heaven appears to be a realm located between Gekai (Earth) and Ten where Jusuheru is allowed to reign and make free use of the fruit of the *masan*. It is a realm of empty space supposedly 8 *chō* (approximately 872 meters) from the earth. By reigning between these realms, Jusuheru's role is clearly one of interference (Kamiya 1986:50). The entry of the three persons who are Jusuheru's doing—Ambition, Covetousness, and Selfishness—emphasizes the dynamic relationship between the realms of Earth and Middle Heaven, demonstrating how *tengu* influence is internalized by humans and thereby spreads like the seed of the *masan* itself.

21. Tagita and Ebisawa cite the hurling of the needle and the comb as allusions to Susa-no-mikoto placing the maiden trans-

formed into a comb in his hair or Izanagi throwing the comb and stick. The Kakure Kirishitan might have known these motifs as part of popular tradition, transmitted by itinerant individuals such as *biwa hōshi* (minstrels) and *kijiya* (woodworkers), who carved, among other things, *biwa* (Kamiya 1986:95).

The key issue here seems to be that of incest. The exchange of the comb and needle is a ritual that breaks the blood tie between brother and sister and thus enables them to become husband and wife according to Christian law. Throughout Japanese history incest seems to have occurred widely, since no laws or religious prohibitions banned consanguinous marriages. When Christianity was introduced to Japan in the mid-sixteenth century, however, marriage even with third cousins was forbidden. By 1918, this prohibition stopped short of second cousins where it remains today. Consanguinous marriages were frequent among the Kirishitan, since their religion had the effect of isolating them in both the Nagasaki area and the Gotō Islands (Schull 1953).

When Petitjean began discovering the ancient Christians in the Nagasaki area, he was disturbed by the similarity of their living arrangements to those of non-Christians. He estimated that one-fourth were living in irregular marital conditions because of divorce. In addition, as the Kirishitan were unwilling to marry unbelievers, many marriages were considered consanguinous as defined by the Catholic church (Cary 1976:289).

22. "Seeing that all things foretold came to pass": the Japanese reads *"koi oshie no tori o mite."* As this sentence is written in hiragana, the interpretation remains open. It could also be translated as "They watched the love-teaching birds." Other critics, including Hayao, prefer this more primordial reading because it echoes the *Nihongi* (I:10) where Izanagi and Izanami are taking their nuptial vow by circling round the heavenly pole. They then witness two birds, a species of pipit, joined and agitated in flight. The heavenly consorts then imitate these "love-teaching birds." In the *Tenchi* the "love-teaching bird" would suggest the sexual act between Chikorō and Tanhō.

23. The increase in the human population, the food shortage

that ensues, and the people turning to God for help constitute a prelude to two myths of origin. The first is the origin of agriculture: God gave humans unhulled rice seed, which they planted and then reaped an abundant harvest. The second is the origin of the *tauta* (sowing songs): a commemoration of this original event or covenant between God and humans in which God helps them survive. While no documents for the planting song *hachi ho hachi koku* seem to exist in Gotō or Sotome, a song with similar elements is found in Fukuoka, where it is associated with a rice planting festival of Kanemura Shrine (Kamiya 1986:82):

> *Aara medeta ya sōrai sōrai*
> *Kotoshi no ine wa*
> *hachi ho de hachi koku*
> *Kyu koku ni nareba*
> *Tono no yo zakari*
> *Honhōya yanho.*

> Oh, what a joy! Sōrai Sōrai!
> This year's rice seedlings
> eight *koku* for eight ears
> when it reaches nine
> our lord will prosper
> Hallelujah!

(A *koku* is 180 liters.)

24. What lower heaven these three evil ones were assigned to is unclear. Although Middle Heaven is not mentioned, that is where Jusuheru reigns, and he is held responsible for unleashing them into the world. Within the Buddhist system the three appear to have gone to Shura, or Ashura, a hell inhabited by the angry. This is likely since Shura is located at the bottom of the ocean surrounding Shumisen (Mount Sumeru)—the silver, gold, and crystal mountain was believed to stand in the center of the world and the sea at its base was thought to contain one of the eight kinds of lowly beings.

25. The topos of a flood that destroys the wicked and saves the righteous few is as ancient and universal as the memory of a lost continent or sunken island with a grandiose legacy. The desire to rediscover such a landmass serves as an impetus to set the quest

motif in action. Thus the memory persists in various cultures: Saint Brendan's Isle, the Fortunate Isles of the Greeks, the Welsh Isle of Avalon, the Portuguese Isle of Seven Cities, Antilia (appearing on maps of the fifteenth and sixteenth centuries), and Lemuria (the Pacific counterpart of Atlantis), better known by its abbreviation Mu (a continent risen to prominence in a few of Japan's New Religions such as Mahikari and Kōfuku no Kagaku).

The oldest Japanese version of this story is found in the *Konjaku Monogatari,* where it is titled "Ouna Mainichi Sotoba ni Chi no Tsuku o Mitaru Koto" (The Old Woman Who Checked the Mortuary Stakes for Blood Every Day) (*Konjaku Monogatari-shū* 1960:334–336). In terms of popular tradition, versions of this motif—in which an island of affluent people sinks into the sea and only the righteous few are spared—are found wherever the Kirishitan settled. The collective authorship of the *Tenchi* incorporated the local version of this widespread legend into the narrative.

In the opinion of a Kakure Kirishtan *mizukata* from Sotome, the origin of the Ariōshima story in the *Tenchi* refers to Ōbe-tō and Kobe-tō, two islands off the coast of Mie on the Nishi-Sonogi peninsula. The smaller of these, Kobe-tō, is said to have sunk; the larger one, Ōbe-tō, is still visible. On a fisherman's map the shoal resulting from the sunken Kobe-tō is called Bettō-zone.

A tale from Tokushima in Shikoku, "Shika no Medama ga Akaku Naru Toki" (When the Deer's Eyes Turn Red), narrates a story parallel to that found in the *Tenchi.* The Gotō Islands have variations of this story. The town of Miraku on Fukuejima has a story of Jizō's face turning red before the island sinks. From the town of Warabi on Hisakajima comes the legend of Koraizone, a sunken landmass in northwestern Gotō. The town still keeps the statue of the Korai-Jizō in a small enclosure in the Buddhist cemetery. On Ukujima, a story is told of Hotoke's mouth turning red before the island sinks. In Gotō these tales are all referred to as the legend of Koraizone.

In Ōita the legend of Uruijima features a statue of Ebisu-sama. In Kagoshima, the legend of Banrigashima revolves around a statue of Jizō-sama. Near Sendai a similar tale is called the legend of

Tagamura (Tani 1987:206–210). For more variations see Inada (1988:259): "Jizō-no-Yokoku" (Jizō's Forewarning) and "Ryūjin no Yokoku" (The Forewarning of the Dragon God). See also Yanagita (1992:532–548) and Tagita (1967).

26. The discrimination against the *noriokuretaru ichi-nin no ani* (the lame son) by his father, Pappa Maruji (Pope-Martyr), his abandonment, and his eventual rescue by miraculous means raise essential questions about attitudes toward the disabled and the role of the divine in Japanese tradition. The psychoanalyst Kawai Hayao, in his discussion of the *Tenchi*, identifies the lame son with the *hiruko*—the leech-child of Japanese myth. The parents of this armless and legless monstrosity, Izanagi and Izanami, throw out this child, their firstborn, by placing it in a reed boat and allowing it to float off to its destiny. In Japanese myth, this is the extent of the child's role. In the *Tenchi* version, however, this myth is Christianized: the child, favored by the divine, is retrieved and restored by supernatural means to human society.

The *hiruko* is sometimes identified with Ebisu, the Japanese god of wealth. Depicted as variously deformed—deaf, one-eyed, left-handed, hermaphroditic, hunchbacked—Ebisu is also worshiped as the god of fishing and later as a god of commerce. According to Jacob Raz: "The word ebisu means: an Ainu, a stranger, a foreigner, a barbarian, or a person from a remote place. Ebisu is thus a god coming from a remote land to bring good luck" (1992:21). The retrieval of the child gives the story a purpose within a scheme of divine grace that is absent in the Shinto system. The story also strongly suggests the story of Moses. Kawai notes that on islands off Kyushu there are shrines dedicated to Ebisu, who is considered the returned *hiruko*. Many spots in Japan exist where the kanji meaning "leech-child" is read locally as "Ebisu," the most widely revered *kami* (Shinto deity) in fishing villages throughout Japan. Delgado reports a shrine in Koshikijima called "Ebisu-Deusu" (Delgado 1985a:68).

27. Ex post facto justifications are a prominent feature of the *Tenchi* narrative. Here *haguro,* the practice of painting the teeth black, and *mayuotosu,* the shaving of eyebrows, are presented as

major necessities in the postdiluvian world in order to curb indis-
criminate sexual practices resulting from the inability to distinguish married from unwedded women.

The custom of blackening the teeth was not imported from
China but seems originally to have entered Japan through migra-
tion of Malaysian people to the archipelago. During the Heian era
(794–858) young girls adopted the practice, and from the twelfth
century noblemen and warriors began to blacken their teeth as
well. Later, during the Tokugawa period, both the shaving of eyebrows and blackening of teeth were forbidden to classless Japanese.
By the latter half of the eighteenth century, blackened teeth indi-
cated marital status and the fidelity of wife to husband. (The practice was expected to be kept up through widowhood.) From a
more pragmatic point of view, the substance used for blackening
was thought to prevent toothaches and generally to protect the
teeth. From 1873 the empress, through her contact with Western
women, decided to quit the practice. Following her precedent, the
practice was considered an anachronism to be found only in
remote parts of Japan among isolated minorities such as the *ebune*
(itinerant boat dwellers).

28. The Trinity—the unity of Father, Son, and Holy Spirit—is
one of the most abstract and perplexing doctrines of Christianity. It
is no surprise, then, that it either suffered a sea change in the
course of its several-hundred-year transmission or else was mis-
understood by the Kakure Kirishitan from the start. The Bible has
no explicit reference to the Trinity, although two verses (Matthew
28:19 and 2 Corinthians 13:14) are often cited as Trinitarian. The
Trinity is above all thought to be revealed in the divine activity of
the New Testament and manifested in Christian experience. Tertul-
lian is credited with first formulating the concept and coining the
words *trinitas, persona,* and *substantia.* His idea was that God was
one but played three distinct roles, since *persona* referred to an
actor's mask. In this case, the drama was that of human redemption. *Substantia* was that which the three persons of the Trinity had
in common. The Trinity, then, was outward diversity and inward
unity. The Kakure Kirishitan interpretation of the Trinity is not

"three persons, one substance." It is dualistic and instead shows God splitting into two autonomous divine persons—Father and Son—after discussing the need for human salvation with his angels who serve as counselors to a God who curiously seems to lack omniscience.

29. According to the Bible, an angel tells Zechariah that his wife Elizabeth will conceive (Luke 1:13). The Archangel Gabriel (Luke 1:26) visits Mary to announce that she has been selected to be the mother of God. Jiwan, the water official in the *Tenchi*, refers to John the Baptist whom Elizabeth conceives at the advanced age of fifty-three and who will baptize Jesus. Jiwan is the archetype of the *mizukata*, or baptizer, among the Kakure Kirishitan and also their god of baptism. The small island of Kabashima in southern Gotō has the only free-standing sanctuary of the Kakure Kirishitan sect in the Gotō Islands: it is devoted to San Jiwan, a foreign catechist who labored underground in the 1650s and ultimately disappeared. Built in the postwar years, on its altar is a large stone with the name San Jiwan carved in kanji, a statue of Kūkai, a cross, and other icons of mixed heritage.

30. Each round of the rosary has three series of five "mysteries" (the joyful, the sorrowful, and the glorious mysteries), or five decades of ten Ave Marias, plus three more at the end before reaching the cross. The total is thus 53. The *Doctrina Christan* refers to both the fiftyfold *rosario-orassho* and the sixty-three *coroa* (small ten-beaded rosary). The Ave Maria (Latin) and the Hail Mary (English) are one and the same prayer.

31. Roson, or Luçon (Luzon), is the largest of the Philippine Islands. During the Christian era many Spanish ships on their way to Mexico began to call at Japanese ports to the displeasure of the Jesuits who had until then exercised a monopoly on trade in Japan. These ships also began to carry Catholic missionaries of the mendicant orders—Franciscans, Augustinians, and Dominicans. In Manila, where these ships originated, the Japanese had several towns *(Nihon-machi)* where their merchants resided and which later became places of refuge, particularly for Christians of noble birth who either fled or were exiled from Japan during the persecutions.

The king's name, Sanzen Zezusu (Three Thousand Jesuses), foreshadows his posthumous role as heavenly spouse of Maruya-sama. This is yet another instance of numerical hyperbole as seen earlier in the description of Deusu. In Japan, the power of a bodi-sattva was often represented in the number of its manifestations: Kyoto's Sanjūsangen-dō with its 1,001 statues of Kannon is yet another example of this tendency.

32. The choice of the name Maruya instead of Mariya or Maria may be due to the fact that *maru* (circle) in Japanese con-veys a sense of roundness or wholeness along with the implication of birth and fertility. *Maru* is a character used as a suffix in ships' names and formerly in the names of swords or indeed anything considered precious. The choice of the name may also have been conditioned by the necessity for secrecy.

33. In Catholicism the age of seven is considered the dawn of moral consciousness.

34. Biruzen (Port. *virgem*): virgin.

35. According to Ebisawa, traces of the Franciscans can be found in certain practices of the Kakure Kirishitan in the Kurosaki area. He cites the custom among Franciscans of the time of saying the Abe Maruya twelve times on Christmas Eve (Ebisawa 1970b: 388). However, twelve is a biblical number par excellence: twelve apostles, twelve sins, twelve gates to New Jerusalem, twelve tribes of Israel, and so forth.

36. In Japan of the sixteenth century, masters of *kōdō* (the incense ceremony) prized an incense they called *jinkō (Aquilaria agallocha)*, known as aloeswood in English. Six varieties of *jinkō* existed and were collectively known as *rikkoku* (six countries), a name based on their diverse countries of origin. Thus the name of a fragrance was also a country's name. *Kyara*, the most exquisite variety of the six, is the only exception, for it means "black" in Sanskrit. It was imported then, as it still is today, from either Cam-bodia or Vietnam. The making of *jinkō* required an aging process by which the trunk of the cut evergreen tree was buried under-ground and the resinous wood was thereby transformed (Morita 1992:53–56).

37. The miracle of the snow falling in August refers to a fourth-century Italian legend according to which an heirless patrician, Giovanni Patricio, beseeched the Virgin to show him where he should put his fortune. The Virgin appeared to him on 5 August 352 and to Pope Liberius (352–366) and urged them to build a church where she would place snow. Although it was summer, the following day snow was found on the Esquiline Hill in Rome—the site where the church of Santa Maria Maggiore was then built. The Kakure Kirishitan celebrate this festival on 4 August, calling it Yuki no Santa Maria (Our Lady of the Snow). A Japanese manuscript dated 1591 and known as the Vatican Reg. Lat. 459 contains many European Christian legends selected from works as notable as the *Legenda Aurea*. Listed among the Marian feasts is Santa Maria ad Nives (Our Lady of the Snow) (Schütte 1940:231). The Kakure Kirishitan reinterpretation of the legend, however, is quite original. Maruya metaphorically represents the Kakure Kirishitan through whom they seem to express their grave sense of oppression under a rich and powerful Tokugawa regime that was forcing them into a "marriage" that conflicted with their own religious commitments.

In the village of Shittsu on the Nishi-Sonogi peninsula, a scroll painting of Yuki no Santa Maria was found in recent years rolled up inside a blackened bamboo pipe. This blonde with a slightly Asian face and a beauty mark on her left cheek is clothed in red and wears a crown of camellias. Thought to have been painted by a native Japanese between 1597 and 1614, the scroll was given to Tanaka Yōjirō by a Kakure Kirishitan family. It is now kept in the Twenty-Six Martyrs Museum in Nagasaki (Tanaka 1984.)

38. The figure of Maruya—both shaman and preteen—is complex and the only developed character in the narrative. This cameo scene with the King of Roson is a standard example of the *tennin nyōbo* (celestial wife) motif in which a supernatural woman enters into a relationship with a mortal man. In the Asian tradition, these celestial maidens *(tennyō* or *tennin)* derive from the Buddhist devas—female deities of India.

As these mixed unions are not between equals, the couple is

destined for separation. A visitor from a supernatural world, the woman eventually yearns to return to her true element. Prior to her departure, however, she typically reveals her supernatural origin and leaves behind some earthly trace: a garment, a teaching, even a child. Such tales of separation end with the human husband seeking his lost love. One well-known Japanese tale employing this motif is *Kaguya hime* (The Shining Princess). Others are *Ko no hana sakuya hime* (The Lady Who Causes Trees to Bloom) and the Nō drama *Hagoromo* (The Robe of Feathers). Since Maruya effectively rejects the king's marriage proposal from the start, this story has a richer texture than a mere celestial wife tale.

The flower wagon that takes Maruya to heaven functions within two traditions. First, it bears a striking resemblance to the *goshoguruma*—the decorated carriages used to carry persons of distinction since the Muromachi period and prior to that associated with imperial outings. Secondly, the entire floral scene is also reminiscent of Mary's assumption when, according to tradition, she rose physically and spiritually to heaven. A legend of the second century purports that the apostles found Mary's tomb empty after her assumption except for flowers strewn around the tomb. In church lore, the aftermath of the same event is often described as a shower of roses and lilies—attributes of sanctity and purity—that fell and filled the empty tomb.

In the Catholic tradition, following the Assumption, Mary is crowned Queen of Heaven by her divine son and receives a crown of twelve stars. This event is known as the Coronation of Mary. Neither the Assumption (15 August) nor the Coronation is recorded in the New Testament. Although the Assumption was not defined as Catholic dogma until 1950 by Pope Pius XII, it nevertheless played a vital role in popular religious belief. It is included in the rosary cycle as the fourth of the glorious mysteries. This appears to be the reason for its inclusion here.

The Kakure Kirishitan depiction of Maruya's ascension to heaven seems to trace a rite of passage. By definition such a rite is marked by a separation and return. It requires a break with the old self or former identity followed by a period of incubatory isolation

in which the initiate is suspended between two phases of being—
past and future—a painful moment of suspension in which one
effectively has no identity. During this ordeal the initiate is finally
marked in some way by the divine. In the Catholic myth, Mary
receives her crown; in the Kakure Kirishitan version, Maruya receives a "rank" and finally emerges with a new status manifested
in her new name: Yuki no Santa Maruya. With this new status she
returns to the old world. Only after this encounter with the divine
—or after a personal religious experience that transforms her—
does she acquire a rank and learn her mission in the world. With
knowledge of this purpose she can return to the world to exercise a
new freedom being in it but no longer of it.

39. The Archangel Gabriel visits Mary to announce that she of
all women has been selected to be the mother of Jesus (Luke 1:26).

40. In the Bible, Mary conceives by the Holy Spirit in the form
of a dove. In Latin the word is *columba,* and in Portuguese,
pomba. Neither of these suggests "Korodo," the name she is given
after she conceives: Korodo no Maruya. In fact, *korodo* probably
derives from the word for "crown"—in Latin, *corona;* in Portuguese, *coroa.* Starting in the sixteenth century, a prayer used in
Japan was called the "Koroha no inori." In praise of the Virgin, it
consisted of saying the Abe Maruya sixty-three times.

The use of the butterfly may derive its meaning from other
associations. In Christianity it represents the resurrection, soul,
psyche, and immortality. These Christian associations themselves
derive from the classical world: in Greek, *psyche* means both butterfly and soul. The butterfly is also a symbol in Buddhism of
Sakyamuni, and in China it is sometimes employed as a symbol of
conjugal felicity and joy. In the *Tenchi* a meshing of these traditions
can be seen.

As a motif in Japanese literature, virgin births, solar births, or
other supernatural births are not uncommon. Sun pregnancy myths
came to Japan from the continent and are widespread among
Mongols, Koreans, and Manchus. The story of Akaru-hime (The
Bright Princess) in the *Kojiki* tells of a woman of humble birth who
is impregnated by sunshine while taking a nap in the nude by a

swamp. She gives birth to a red jewel that later becomes a princess (Philippi 1989:291–293). Tagita too notes a legend of Toyotomi Hideyoshi's birth in which his mother conceives after the sun jumps into her mouth (Tagita 1966:3:115).

41. In the biblical story, Mary travels to the uplands of Judah to meet Elizabeth. When they meet, Mary's greeting stirs the child inside Elizabeth and Mary remains three months with her friend (Luke 1:39). In the *Tenchi* narrative the two women, seemingly in telepathic communication, set out to meet each other. The words uttered by Elizabeth in the Kakure Kirishitan text are the basis of the well-known prayer Hail Mary, which sums up all the Catholic theology concerning Mary and contains both praise and petition. The Archangel Gabriel says to Mary, "Hail, full of grace, the Lord is with thee; blessed art thou among women" (Luke 1:28). Elizabeth says to Mary, "Blessed art thou among women and blessed is the fruit of thy womb" (Luke 1:42). The Catholic church then added the petitionary invocation, "Holy Mary, mother of God, pray for us sinners now, and at the hour of our death. Amen." Mary's response in the *Tenchi* closely resembles another prayer, the Our Father.

42. Their encounter takes place at the Abe River, which is offered as an explanation of the origin of the Abe Maruya (Ave Maria) prayer. Tagita suggests the Kakure Kirishitan took the river's name from the battle site where the Heike and Genji clans fought. Abe is also a name of a river in Akita located in an area where Christian popular tradition claims both Hebrew and Christian roots.

43. This scene suggests derivation from the popular tradition of noncanonical or apocryphal works. Although Joseph does not figure in the *Tenchi* narrative, a comparable scene and parallel sentiment are found in the Infancy Gospel, the Protevangelium of James, in which the discovery of Mary's pregnancy gives rise to Joseph's accusations of promiscuity: "Why have you humiliated your soul, you who were brought up in the Holy of Holies and received food from the hand of an angel? . . . Whence then is this in your womb?" (Cullman 1973:381). This gospel was translated by

Gion (Guillaume) Postel (1510–1581), one of the most brilliant linguists of his day, who was a Jesuit for a brief period. His Latin translation, published in 1552, was condemned by the pope and the Roman church, although it was highly venerated in the Greek church.

Popular noncanonical traditions formed the substance of Jacobus de Voragine's *Legenda Sanctorum* (Readings on the Saints), circa 1260, a book whose popularity throughout Europe was second only to the Bible during the Middle Ages (Ryan 1993:xiii–xviii). Parts of this work were translated into Japanese by an unknown author, probably supervised by the Jesuit Pero Ramón. The work is known by the Portuguese Jesuit who copied it, Manuel Barreto. The manuscript (Vatican Reg. Lat. 459) consists of nearly four hundred folios of Japanese paper. Besides the European hagiography and Japanese Christian legends, it contains instructional guidance for Japanese priests (Schütte 1940:226–280; 1962:3–29).

44. Beren (Port. *Berem*): Bethlehem.

45. *Zeshin* (Port. *jejum*): fasting.

46. Mary gives birth to Jesus in the stable among the animals. This nativity scene, so often depicted in Western art, is found not in the Bible but in a noncanonical work—the Apocryphal Infancy Gospel of Matthew. According to this gospel, an angel leads Mary into a dark cave that is suddenly illuminated when the Virgin gives birth to Jesus. On the third day they leave the cave and enter a stable where the holy infant is put in a manger. There an ox and donkey worship the child (Hall 1990:127; Cullman 1973:410). The warmth of the animals' breath that saves the newborn from freezing appears to be an original addition in the *Tenchi*. Stephen Turnbull (1996:70) first drew my attention to this Infancy Gospel.

An integral part of Otaiya—the Kakure Kirishitan celebration of Christ's nativity (23 December)—is its focus on the efforts of On Haha Santa Maruyasama. A fast is observed from the moment of gathering until midnight, when it is broken with a feast. A manuscript by Mitsuzō Iwamura dated 1972 and titled "Warera no Shūkyō" (Our Religion) offers the following description of how to perform the service:

The evening gathering begins around 6 P.M. The ritual *chikara-zoe* (prayers of encouragement) are offered to Santa Maru-yasama and to Izaberiyasama. Offerings are made to two deities. The *ochikarazoe orassho* are said 365 times. They are divided into three sittings. At the first sitting, they are said 130 times to each deity. Afterwards, at the closing, offerings are made to Santa Maruyasama and to Izaberiyasama.

The second sitting is at midnight. The *oyorokobi* prayer and an offering are made to On Haha Santa Maruyasama and to Anatasama Onmenyosusama. The third or dawn sitting begins around 7 A.M. Offerings are made to Anatasama Onmen-yosusama and to On Haha Santa Maruyasama.

The birth-inducing *ochikarazoe* prayer from Maruya's perspective seems to refer to her sentiments at the Annunciation itself. It is reproduced here with my translation:

> *Yume mitari, yume yutari. Yosusama awaremi tamae awaremi tamae. Anmen Yosu katajikenai.*

(In a dream I saw, in a dream I heard. Jesus have mercy have mercy on me. Amen Jesus. Thanks be to thee.)

47. Weekly fasts are still observed by a handful of Kakure Kiri-shitan on Wednesday, Friday, and Saturday. The only time in the Kakure Kirishitan calendar that traditionally required a fast, however, was from Haritsuke (28 February) until Kanashimiagari (15 April): during this period the eating of meat and eggs was forbidden. This practice was observed in gratitude toward the animals whose warm breath kept the Christ child alive in the cold stable.

48. Turnbull (1996:69) traces the source of this story to the Arabic Infancy Gospel. According to this gospel, a woman took sweet-smelling water and washed Jesus' feet with it. She then kept this water and poured some of it on the body of a leprous girl who was cleansed of her disease (Cullman 1973:408).

49. *Shirukushisan* (Port. *circumçisão*): circumcision.

50. The origin of this story of the three kings or astrologers on their way to worship the savior is found in the Bible (Matthew 2:1), and in Christianity it is often referred to as the Adoration of

the Magi. In the *Tenchi* the three kings are Menteo of Turkey, Gasuparu of Mexico, and Bautozaru of France (all fairly common Portuguese names). Three notable Jesuit missionaries bore these names: Melchior Nuñez (d. 1571), Gaspar Vilela (1525–1572), and Balthazar Gago (1515–1583). In the Apocryphal Armenian Infancy Gospel, however, a remarkable correspondence is found. This gospel contains the contents of the Protevangelium of James with further elaborations. One of these is the Magi depicted as three royal brothers: Melqon of Persia, Balthasar of India, and Gaspar of Arabia (Cullman 1973:405). The three countries named, however, are different in the *Tenchi*. Although the reason for this is unclear, Turkey, Mexico, and France were known to the Japanese of this era for different reasons. In the case of Mexico, ships began to sail there from Manila in the beginning of the seventeenth century. Turkey was known for the Battle of Lepanto (1571), a naval clash between allied Christian forces and the Ottoman Turks over the possession of Cyprus. The victory of the Christians had a tremendous impact on European morale and was the subject of paintings by such notables as Titian and Tintoretto. The subject even turned up in a painting done in Japan by a native painter in Western style, although the sea battle was transferred to land. (For a reproduction see Cooper 1971:178.) From France there appears to have been but one Jesuit who came to Japan: Theodoro Manteles (1560–1593) (Frois 1984:5:101). After Portugal and Spain, the majority of missionaries were from the Italian peninsula; the remainder came from Poland and Flanders (Matsuda 1993:19).

51. Yorotetsu is Herod of the Bible.

52. The bridge with three different paths that hung suspended from heaven is referred to as *ten no tsurihashi*. In the *Nihongi,* the Japanese history of creation, the expression used is *ame no ukihashi* (floating bridge of heaven). As in earlier Kojikian elements, such images probably entered the popular imagination and do not refer to any significant or sustained allusion to these classical works.

53. The Roman governor Pontius Pilate becomes two people in the *Tenchi*—Ponsha and Piroto—the vassals of Yorotetsu.

54. This episode of Maruya and the Holy One's flight into

Egypt and encounter with the wheat sowers is similar to an apocryphal story widespread during the Middle Ages. According to this story, Mary and Jesus were fleeing from Herod's soldiers when they met a peasant who was sowing wheat. Jesus reached into the man's sack, took out a handful of wheat, and threw the seeds on the ground. At that moment wheat sprang up and stood as high and ripe as if the summer were at its close. When Herod's soldiers approached and asked the peasant if he had seen a woman with a child, the man answered, "Oh, yes, when I sowed this wheat I saw them." Hearing this and observing the ripened wheat, the soldiers turned around and gave up their search (Longnon and Cazelles 1973:182).

Alfred Bohner notes that other legends of similar theme are told in relation to Kūkai Kōbō Daishi, such as the legends "Kuwazu-imo" (Bitter Potatoes) and "Kuwazu-nashi" (Bitter Pears) (Bohner 1938:497). In the first legend, from Ōita, Kūkai meets a woman carrying a load of potatoes on her shoulder and asks her to share some with him. But she refuses him saying that she washed them in a deep river—implying both the trouble and the risk of the task—and invents the excuse that they are bitter and unpalatable. Kūkai goes to the river and finds it shallow. With his staff he scrapes the bottom, making the river deep and the potatoes acrid. In the second story, from Shikoku, Kūkai goes to a place where people are gathering pears. They refuse to give him any with the excuse that they are unpalatable. Kūkai then renders the pears of the trees tasteless. See *Kaitei Sōgō Nippon Minzoku Goi* (1955:510).

In 1992 on the island of Kabashima I met a Kakure couple. Although they had never heard of the *Tenchi Hajimari no Koto* as such, later in our conversation, when I asked them if they knew any local legends, the woman spontaneously told this story of wheat sowers as rendered in the *Tenchi*.

55. Here the sight of Jesus' baptism in the River Jordan shifts location to a big river called Bauchisumo (Port. *bautismo*), or "baptism." After Jesus is baptized by San Jiwan he is known as Jusukiri (Port. *Jesu Christo*). The term *christo*, meaning "the anointed one,"

was actually a title bestowed on new priests who were anointed with oil. Christ's baptism is told in the Bible (Matthew 3:13).

In the *Tenchi,* the dividing of the waters into forty thousand rivers is original. In a less visual context, however, the Bible expresses the same idea: "Go forth to every part of the world, and proclaim the Good News to the whole creation. Those who believe it and receive baptism will find salvation; those who do not believe will be condemned" (Mark 16:16).

56. Taboro, from the biblical Mount Tabor, was the site where Jesus' transfiguration occurred in the presence of apostles Peter, James, and John (Matthew 17:1). In the *Tenchi* Jesus ascends to heaven, meets God face-to-face, and receives a "rank" and a crown there.

57. Zeze-Maruya (Port. *Gethsemania*) refers to Gethsemane, a plot of land on the Mount of Olives in Jerusalem where an oil press was located and where Jesus used to meet with his disciples. He later suffered his Agony there and was arrested (Mark 14:32; Matthew 26:36).

58. After Jesus receives a rank following his encounter with God on Mount Tabor, he is then ordained. He begins his studies on the fiftieth day under the tutelage of Sagaramento (Port. *sacramento*), or "sacrament," who descends from heaven and remains a full week. In the Kakure Kirishitan calendar, two holy days are observed that do not have names but are referred to as "Forty Days After the End of Mourning" and "Fifty Days After the End of Mourning." The End of Mourning is equivalent to Easter. Jesus' ascension in the *Tenchi,* therefore, seems to be confused with the Easter occurring the third day after his death. Thus the crucifixion is observed as Kanashimi no iri ("entering into mourning") on 28 February, and Kanashimi no agari ("lifting of mourning") is observed on 15 April (Iwamura 1972:1–2).

The number 12 appears again as the age until which Jesus pursues his studies. Earlier in the *Tenchi,* Maruya began her studies at age seven and received her calling and vow at age twelve also. In the Bible, Jesus is twelve when his parents discover he is missing and find him among scholars in a temple of Jerusalem (Luke 2:41).

59. In the *Tenchi* reference is actually made to the five "articles." I have translated these as "five mysteries of the morning" (page 54), the "five mysteries of the day" (page 57), and the "five mysteries of the evening" (page 62), because they are explicit references to the Catholic rosary and the religious mysteries it represents. By "mysteries" is meant something both sacred and difficult to understand. As a structure the rosary is composed of five groups of ten beads called "decades" on which the prayer Hail Mary is to be said. Each decade is preceded by a separate bead on which is said an Our Father. A complete recitation of the rosary, however, consists of fifteen decades: recitation of the entire rosary three times. It is thus a total of 150 "roses" with each complete rosary devoted to each group of mysteries: joyful, sorrowful, and glorious. The rosary is in effect a compendium of the life of Jesus and Mary and a summary of the Catholic liturgical year.

The prayers are counted on the beads as an instrument to assist the memory. Since recitation of the rosary three times is quite time consuming, it was customary to divide its recitation into three parts to be recited at a different times of the day. One rosary manual states: "I advise you to divide up your rosary into three parts and to say each group of mysteries (five decades) at a different time of day. This is much better than saying the whole fifteen decades all at once" (De Montfort 1991:95). This tripartite division is precisely the structure found in the *Tenchi*. The morning refers to the five joyful mysteries, the daytime to the five sorrowful mysteries, and the evening to the five glorious mysteries.

The missionaries of the sixteenth and seventeenth centuries working in Japan—particularly the Franciscan, Dominican, and Augustinian friars—were fond of giving rosaries and holy medals to their converts. The Jesuits, having been in Japan some fifty years before the arrival of the other groups, had learned to be more cautious, although both Saint Ignatius Loyola, founder of the Jesuit order, and Saint Francis Xavier were themselves deeply devoted to the rosary.

The rosary was a potent series of tableaux or snapshot images designed to inspire and guide the faithful. As a prayer technique it exploited the visual, vocal, and tactile. Another name for the rosary was the "Psalter of Jesus and Mary," since it contained the same number of angelic salutations (Hail Marys) as there are psalms in the Book of David (150). The rosary was intended especially for illiterate people who were unable to read the psalms directly from the Bible.

The first series of mysteries that the rosary treats is the joyful mysteries—so named for the joy these events are thought to have brought into the world. In contemplative circles, they relate to the purgative life:

> 1. Annunciation: The Angel Gabriel comes to Mary (Luke 1:26).
> 2. Visitation: Mary visits Elizabeth (Luke 1:39).
> 3. Nativity: Mary goes to Bethlehem (Luke 2:6).
> 4. Presentation in the temple: Visit to Jerusalem (Luke 2:22).
> 5. Finding of Jesus in the temple: Jesus is with the scholars in the temple (Luke 2:42).

The second series is the sorrowful mysteries. These correspond spiritually to the illuminative life:

> 1. Agony in the garden: Jesus stays in the Garden of Olives, Gethsemane (Matthew 26:36).
> 2. Scourging: Jesus is handed over to Pilate (Mark 15:1).
> 3. Crowning: Soldiers dress Christ in a purple robe and twist some thorns into a crown (John 19:2).
> 4. Carrying the cross: Christ leaves the city carrying his cross (John 19:17).
> 5. Crucifixion: Reaching the place called Calvario ("Skull"), Christ is crucified (Luke 23:33).

The third series, the glorious mysteries, refers to the unitive spiritual life:

1. Resurrection: After removing the stone, an angel reports to the apostles that no one is there and Christ has risen (Matthew 28:5).
2. Ascension: Christ ascends to heaven (Acts 1:3).
3. Pentecost: The Holy Spirit is sent to the apostles as tongues of fire (Acts 2:3).
4. Assumption: Mary is adorned with the sun and stands on the moon (Revelation 12:1).
5. Crowning: Mary is crowned Queen of Heaven and wears a crown of twelve stars.

The life of Jesus and Mary in the *Tenchi* matches the meditations of the first two sets of the rosary: the joyful and the sorrowful mysteries. The glorious mysteries typically receive cursory treatment—probably due to their higher level of abstraction, for the Kakure Kirishitan prefer concrete imagery in their religion.

60. The origin of the name Barandō is unclear. The last syllable, *-dō,* is a suffix meaning "sanctuary" or "chapel." The name Gakujūran derives from *gakushora,* meaning "Buddhist teachers." The dispute that follows draws from Christian and Buddhist traditions. In Christian tradition, Jesus argues with the Jewish elite in the temple and, later, the Apostle Paul in Athens confronts the Epicureans and the Stoics. In the Apocryphal Infancy Gospel of Thomas, Christ is depicted as an enfant terrible who outshines all his teachers, one of whom remarks: "I strove to get a disciple, and have found myself with a teacher" (Cullman 1973:395). In Japan such disputations of priests in the Middle Ages such as Kūkai and Saichō were a common feature of the religious life.

In the Christian era, too, such disputes were widespread. One notable debate took place between the Jesuit Luis Frois and the Buddhist Nichijō Shōnin over the nature of the soul and the Christian God. Frois relates the incident as follows: " 'You say that the soul remains, but you must show it to me now,' he shouted. 'So I'm going to cut off the head of your disciple here (this was Lourenço, who was close to me) so that you can show me the substance that remains.' 'I have already said many times that it isn't a thing that can be seen with the eyes of the body,' I answered." (See Cooper 1965:377–379.) This incident ends with the enraged Shōnin seizing Nobunaga's halberd *(naganata)*, but he is stopped by Nobunaga and dismissed for his discourtesy.

61. Namu-Amida-Butsu ("I take my refuge in Amida Buddha") is a formula prayer known also as the Nembutsu. It was a fundamental practice of Pure Land Buddhism (Jōdo-shū). Indeed, its recitation alone was thought to be an essential key to ensuring birth in the Pure Land and attaining Buddhahood there.

62. *Guzei-no-fune* (Boat of Vows) is a Buddhist term. The original vow of Amida Buddha is compared to a boat that lets people cross over the deep sea of confusion to the shore of satori: enlightenment. Likewise, the four vows of Buddhism can carry people across this perilous sea to the other shore. These four tenets are: Buddha saves humankind everywhere; Buddha knows that human suffering is endless; Buddha's teachings are wide and deep; Buddha's way is the most superior anywhere. This boat metaphor is especially popular in the Jōdo Shin (True Pure Land) sect, and it appears in some of the *wasan,* or Buddhist psalms. I have translated one of them:

> *Shōji no kukai hotori nashi*
> *hisashiku shizumeru warera o ba*
> *Mida Guzei no fune nomi zo*
> *nosete kanarazu watashikeru.*

> Our sea of suffering has no shore
> how long we sink in this sea
> only in Buddha's Boat of Vows
> can we cross over.
> [*Jōdo Shinshū Seiten* 1988:19]

63. According to Buddhist theology, after death one is assigned to one of the six realms (heavens) according to one's sins or behavior in this life. The lowest of these heavens is Jikoku (hell), which contains both a hot and a cold part. This hell, however, differs fundamentally from its Christian counterpart since it is not eternal. A person can gain merit in the Buddhist Jikoku and thereby rise out of it and to a higher heaven. The other heavens are: Gaki (hungry

ghost realm), Chikushō (animal realm), Shura (violent realm), Ningen (human realm), and Tennin (god realm).

64. The universe is measured in *jō,* which is the size of one tatami mat, or 3.314 yards.

65. A *ri* is 2.44 miles. This passage on the near destruction of the island by a typhoon stopped only by the Buddha's intervention is reminiscent of the earlier flood disaster and suggestive of the Book of Revelation.

66. After Gakujūran's twelve disciples become the Holy One's disciples, they are baptized and enter into the sacred relation of master and disciple. They then serve as Konesoru (Port. *confessor*), confessors at Barandō.

67. *Issai-kyō* is a collection of all the sacred scriptures of Buddhism.

68. This is the first mention of Rome (Port. Roma). Santa Ekirenja (Lat. *Santa Ecclesia* or Port. *Santa Igreja*) is the Holy Church of Rome. This part is a confusion of the biblical tradition, for Christ and his disciples did not go to Rome. Only Peter went to lay the foundations of the Catholic church there.

69. In Japan, too, a person is considered a child up to seven years of age. Thus Yorotetsu orders the deaths of all children up to the age of seven. The *Tenchi*'s rendition of Herod's killing of the innocents is magnified through the use of the number 44,444. In Japanese, the number 4 is an unlucky number, as its *on-yomi* (Chinese) pronunciation is *"shi,"* a homophone for the word "death." Thus both the large number and the heinousness of the deed are reinforced through the repetition. For numerical repetitiveness and hyperbole, see note 31. Tagita affirms this supposition, referring to the Thirty-Three Bay Temple in Kyoto said to contain 33,333 images of Buddha (Tagita 1967:67).

70. See note 59.

71. In Japan, miso soup is generally eaten for breakfast and at other meals as well. In the Bible when the disciples ask Jesus which one of them will betray him, he says: " 'It is the man to whom I give this piece of bread when I have dipped it in the dish.' Then, after dipping it in the dish, he gave it to Judas son of Simon

Iscariot" (John 13:26). In the *Tenchi,* Judas betrays Christ on a Wednesday after a breakfast in which he eats his rice with soup. This incident is one of the reasons why some Kakure Kirishitan communities observe a fast on Wednesdays.

72. This episode of Judas' betrayal and his transformation into what appears to be a *tengu* shows how he quite literally "lost face" when he met the apostles, who reproach him for his changed state and what it implies. He hangs himself in the *Tenchi* as he does in the Bible.

73. "That is the origin of the money mound beside the temple of Santa Ekirenja": from Matthew 27:3–10:

> When Judas the traitor saw that Jesus had been con-demned, he was seized with remorse, and returned the thirty silver pieces to the chief priests and elders. "I have sinned," he said; "I have brought an innocent man to this death." But they said, "What is that to us? See to that yourself." So he threw the money down in the temple and left them, and went and hanged himself.
>
> Taking up the money, the chief priests argued: "This can-not be put into the temple fund; it is blood-money." So after conferring they used it to buy the Potter's Field, as a burial-place for foreigners. This explains the name "Blood Acre," by which that field has been known ever since; and in this way fulfilment was given to the prophetic utterance of Jeremiah: "They took the thirty silver pieces, the price set on a man's head (for that was his price among the Israelites), and gave the money for the potter's field, as the Lord directed me." [*New English Bible* 1972:39]

74. In this passage, the exceedingly hot infernal fires of two traditions combined are rising up from the earth: the fire of Naraku (Skt. *Naraka*) is the Indian equivalent of the Japanese Jikoku; Inuheruno (Port. *inferno*) is the Christian hell.

75. This scene of the flagellation and crowning of Jesus is quite close to the biblical version, where he is taken into a courtyard (Mark 15:16). In the *Tenchi,* the beating with a bamboo pole re-turns us to Japan.

76. The placing of bitter and spicy substances in the Holy One's mouth corresponds to the wine mixed with gall that he is offered in the biblical story while he is hanging on the cross (Matthew 27:34).

77. Yorotetsu orders a structure (a cross) with a "length of thirty-three" to be built. The choice of the number may refer to the age of Jesus when he was crucified. He carries this up Karuwaryu Hill (Port. *Calvario*), Calvary. Calvario is a translation of the hill in the Bible where Christ was crucified—Golgotha, meaning "skull" (Mark 15:22).

78. *Sanchiishima* (Lat. *Sanctissima*), the Holiest, here becomes a place with the Japanese suffix for island, *-shima*, added.

79. "In a place called Sanchiishima an enormous tree called the Kurusu-no-ki (Port. *Árvore da Cruz*), the Cross Tree, grows": Symbolizing sacrifice and redemption in Christian art, the cross is often depicted as a living tree. Being mutilated and crucified on a tree and then resurrected is an ancient motif. The Cross Tree is the inversion of the Tree of Life or Tree of Paradise. In the Middle Ages it was sometimes depicted as Y-shaped with living branches. Like the Tree of Life, the cross stands for the "world axis" set at the mystic center of the cosmos and by means of it the soul is thought able to reach God. In the seventh century Christ was represented as the Hanging God on the Tree of Life (Cirlot 1978:69).

Ironically, death by crucifixion was unknown to the Japanese prior to the introduction of Christianity. It then became a common form of execution for those guilty of heinous crimes. To serve as a warning to Christians, victims were sometimes left hanging on the cross for up to a year. In the Japanese method of crucifixion nails were not used. Instead victims were attached to the cross with iron rings and ropes tied around the waist and neck. Francisco Carletti saw the bodies of twenty-six Christians on crosses at Nagasaki in February of 1597:

> These crosses were made like that on which our Redeemer was crucified, though in some respects slightly different from the fashion in which that is usually represented, as they have an additional piece of wood projecting from the front of the stem or trunk of the cross, near the middle, which

helps to support the body of the sufferer, who is seated astride it. Moreover, they have a crosspiece of wood at the bottom to which the feet are tied with the legs apart. And instead of nails they use a sort of iron manacles, which are fixed to the wood of the cross and then wound around the wrists, the neck and the legs near the ankle-bone; or else they tie the aforesaid parts of the body to the cross with cords.

And when in one fashion or the other, they carry out the sentence, the cross is laid on the ground and the body of the sufferer is stretched upon and fixed to it. Then the cross is quickly raised, and its foot being placed in a hole made for the purpose, they prop it up to make it stand firm. This done, the judge who pronounced the sentence who is obliged to be present at its execution, gives the executioner his orders, in accordance with which he pierces the sufferer's body with a spear, thrusting it into the right side upwards through the heart and out above the left shoulder, thus passing through the whole body from one side to the other. [Cooper 1981:156–157]

When combat photojournalist Felice Beato came to Japan in 1863, he turned his talent to photographing the novelties of Japan then in vogue in Europe. Some of his most sensational photos were those of crucifixions and decapitations—forms of execution obsolete in the West that reinforced the image of a bizarre Orient (Edel and Coverdale 1986:88).

80. "Beronica" is Veronica, the water-carrying woman of Samaria who offers Christ water while he staggers up the road on the way to his crucifixion. Although the story of Veronica is not found in the Bible, it was nevertheless a widespread Italian legend that came to be station number six when the stations of the cross were finally standardized to fourteen. These stations depict episodes on Christ's walk up to Calvary in the form of carvings or pictures before which the faithful can meditate.

The legend of Veronica is found in a late Latin addition to the Gospel of Nicodemus: a woman wipes the sweat from Christ's face with her handkerchief as he stumbles up the hill, and his image remains on her cloth. This is the origin of the name Veronica (Lat. *vera icon,* "the true image"). The woman then gives the cloth to

Pope Clement and it comes to be considered one of the three sacred relics of the church and has been kept in Rome since the eighth century. In the *Tenchi* story, Beronica gives the cloth to the Santa Ekirenja (Lat. *Santa Ecclesia*) (Metford 1983:252–253). This legend may well have been transmitted to the Kirishitan by any of the four missionary groups in Japan, but the Franciscans in particular were responsible for popularizing this legend in Europe as well as fostering the practice of praying at the stations of the cross.

81. Jesus is crucified along with two thieves on either side of him (Luke 23:39). The thief on his right, who proclaims Jesus' innocence, is the one who bathed in Jesus' first-bath water and was cured of Hansen's disease. Although this episode does not figure in the biblical story, Stephen Turnbull (1996:70) notes this connecting of the Nativity and Passion as the legend of Saint Dismas (the good thief) and Gestas (the unrepentant thief). Both are named in the Acts of Pilate. While there is no connection between the girl cured of Hansen's disease in the Arabic Infancy Gospel, Jesus makes a prophecy after he and his mother have been accosted by robbers along the road: he tells Mary that he will be crucified in thirty years in Jerusalem with these two robbers (Cullman 1973:408).

82. In Chapter 6 of the *Tenchi* there were only twelve disciples. That the number has almost quadrupled shows the success of the religion.

83. Go-passho (Lat. *Passio;* Port. *Paixao*), the Passion Prayer, is the prayer Christ is thought to have said on the Mount of Olives. (*Go-* is an honorific prefix.) The prayer as said by the Kakure Kirishitan is a summary of Christ's sufferings. Tagita 1978:145 collected a version of this prayer in Kurosaki.

84. This episode in which the blind man gives Christ the death blow for money appears original, since the Bible shows Jesus curing blind men and not being betrayed by them (Matthew 9:27, 20:29; Mark 8:22; Luke 18:35; John 9:1).

85. This episode of Mary crying over the body of Christ is strongly suggestive of a picture of the Pietà that the Kakure Kirishitan may well have seen or perhaps even owned.

86. The burial of Christ in the biblical version occurs on the horizontal plane—the grave is carved into a cave (Matthew 27:60) —and not the Japanese way, which is to dig a vertical hole in the ground.

87. Kirinto (Lat. *Credo*) is a prayer that expresses the Catholic articles of faith. It is found in the sixth chapter of the *Doctrina Christan*. In Gotō this prayer is called Kerendo. A rendition from the village of Obayashi on Narushima is reproduced here:

> Banji. Kanai tamau. Onoya. Jusu. Girisuto sono on-hitori go. Onaraseba. Giritsu. Suberistu Sanchi no. Go-wareki o motte. Yadorase. Tamou. Tokoroe. Berochin no. Santa Mariya-sama Yoku. Umare. Sashi tamau. Unshaberiya. Tetsu ga shita ni. Kasha wao. Uchikorai. Kurosu ni kakari shi. Shishi tamau. Inshi no. Mikaso ni osamenagara. Daiji na. Soko ni. Kudarase tamasan nichi meniwa uomigayarase tamou. Ten ni agarase. Tamai. Banji kanai tamou. Orusu. Sono on migi ni. Sonawa-rase tamai. Sore yorri wa. Ikitaru hito. Shishi taru hito. Tada-shi. Tamoun. Tame ni. Amakudarase tamau. Furuya. Touru ya. Santa Ikirinja-sama. Santasu me ni. Toryoshi tamau tokoro e. Toga no onyurushi ni. Nikushin ni. Yomi ka yarase tamai. Ma-koto ni. Owannaku. Inochi o. Shinji tatematsuru. Amen Josu kadajukenai. [Copied from Fukushima Kumagorō's *orassho* notebook]

88. See note 59.

89. The head disciple—Pappa—is the Pope who meets Christ at the Gate of Virtue. The Holy One remains for forty days to teach Pappa about salvation and the afterlife. Over a period of forty days after Easter, Jesus appeared to his apostles (Abosutoro) and taught them about the kingdom of God (Acts 1:3). The Kakure observe the fortieth day after Easter but have no special name for it. In the Catholic church the fortieth day after Easter is commemorated as Ascension Day (Acts 1:9). In the *Tenchi* the Holy One returns to heaven on the fiftieth day; the Kakure also observe this day as a holy one although it too has no special name. In the Catholic tradition, the fiftieth day after Easter or the tenth day after Christ's Ascension is Pentecost (Acts 2:1), when Christ sent the Holy Spirit in the form of tongues of fire to the apostles.

90. In the *Tenchi*, Maruya ascends to heaven from the Mount of Olives. This would be the actual feast day of the Assumption of Mary, an event the Bible does not record. It is in fact Jesus who in the biblical tradition ascends to heaven from the Mount of Olives. While all bodies are believed to rise from the dead at the end of the world, Mary's body is considered exempt from such corruption by rising in anticipation of the event. Some Kakure groups may have celebrated this day on 3 July.

91. Here the Trinity is once again confused—this time it is divided into three persons with Maruya synonymous with the Holy Spirit, the third person of the Trinity. Jesus as Savior and Deusu as Paateru (Lat. *Pater*) are the other two. This substitution of Mary in place of the Holy Spirit is a departure from Catholic doctrine. As in Chapter 3 of the *Tenchi*, Deusu is not three persons in one but one person who split into three.

92. In Chapter 1 of the *Tenchi*, Koroteru was the equivalent of Eden, but since the Fall it seems to have been transformed into an equivalent of the Limbo of Catholic tradition. Limbo houses those souls eternally excluded from heaven because of original sin since they died without the sacrament of baptism. In Dante's *Inferno*, Limbo is the home of the unbaptized as well as pagans who lived nobly but were born before the coming of Christ. The Kakure Kirishitan too confronted the missionaries with their concern for their ancestors who died before the message of Christianity was brought to Japan. The concept of Limbo effectively confirms the doctrine of the necessity of baptism. Thus the Holy One gives the infants names in the *Tenchi*—presumably baptismal names that will allow their entry to paradise.

93. Beronica obtains the rank of Aneisuteru (Lat. *Agnus Dei*), the "Lamb of God."

94. Saint Michael the Archangel, here San Migiri, is represented variously in Christian art. Although usually depicted with a long spear and standing with a dragon underfoot, he is sometimes portrayed as judge of the dead and weigher of souls at the Last Judgment. In this capacity he holds the scales of judgment in one hand (Whone 1977:110). The *Tenchi* has San Migiri hold a *ban-no-shūken*. Precisely what kind of weapon this might be is unclear,

since only the last syllable of the word is in kanji. *Bannō* can mean "omnipotent" and *shūken* is a short knife. Ebisawa interprets it as a *chōken,* or "long sword"; Tagita, as a "dart."

95. Jurisharen (Port. Jerusalem).

96. Furukatoriya (Port. *Purgatorio*) is a place where those guilty of slight sins or those who have not finished atoning for grave sins must go to do penance before they are worthy of entering heaven. Souls are purified and refined there (Matthew 5:26).

97. Both suicides and murderers go to hell as a matter of course. The Catholic church considers suicide an infraction of the fifth commandment: Thou shalt not kill (Wisdom 16:13). Since life is a gift from God who has dominion over both life and death, suicide is an attempt to usurp God's power. Suicides are not permitted to receive ecclesiastical burial.

98. According to Catholic tradition, San Peitoro (Saint Peter) keeps the keys to the Kingdom of Heaven (Matthew 16:19). There is no Gate-Opening Orassho in Catholic tradition, but Kakure Kirishitan have a funeral tradition according to which they cut a tiny swatch, called *omiyage-mono,* from the martyr Bastian's dark blue kimono, which each village keeps. Formerly this swatch was referred to as *Bastian-sama no kimono no kogire* (Tani 1987:220). This they place in the folded hands of the deceased as a kind of passport that identifies Kakure Kirishitan in the other world and thereby facilitates their entry to paradise.

99. San Pauro (Saint Paul) here is the great discerner of sins. This is an original conception of the saint, for he does not have this role in the Catholic tradition.

100. San Jiwan (Saint John) here inspects, the Abosutoro (the apostles) forgive, and through Santosu the Mediator (the communion of saints) humans will reach Paraiso (Paradise).

101. The end of the world as seen in the *Tenchi* echoes that found in the Book of Revelation with its repetitions of the numbers 3, 7, and 12.

102. Here the fruit of the *masan* becomes extremely dangerous, for it is divested of its shape as an apple and has acquired the power to assume any shape necessary to seduce humans.

103. This adds a tender and pathetic touch: the notion that animals too are hoping for their salvation and resurrection the only way they deem possible—to be eaten by humans and thus become part of that flesh which will be resurrected. In Catholic doctrine animals do not have immortal souls and thus are excluded from the resurrection.

104. Here Santosu blows his shell trumpet (Port. *trombeta*) signaling the resurrection of all bodies. This shell trumpet resembles the *horagai* or conch shell trumpet now associated with the *yamabushi,* the mystic-ascetics who conduct rigorous spiritual practices in mountains considered sacred. The *horagai* was also used in the manner of a church bell by Christians to round up people for mass. In the biblical tradition this blast likewise signals the resurrection and judgment (Revelation 8:7).

105. The practice of cremation was introduced to Japan along with Buddhism in the sixth century. Prior to that time, neither cremation nor the concept of paradise existed in Japan. Shintoism had long considered death a form of pollution and practiced burial of the corpse. By the end of the Heian period (794–1192) the attitude toward death had changed, and it was seen as a necessary stepping stone to Buddha's paradise. In the West, too, burial was not a universal practice among the Greeks and Romans, although the Jews did bury their dead. Christian burial practices followed the Jewish model. Gradually this practice became a fixed convention and then an inviolable law within the Catholic church.

Boniface VIII (pontiff 1294–1303), who had asserted that no article of faith would be jeopardized by cremation, qualified his statement to the effect that the act was still an abomination to God. According to Canon 1203 it was unlawful for a Catholic to carry out the order of anyone who directed that his body be cremated. Canon 1240 stated that those who order their bodies to be cremated, and have not retracted this order prior to death, are deprived of ecclesiastical burial. Finally in Canon 2339, the ultimatum had arrived: anyone who dared to command a competent authority to give Christian burial to someone who had been cremated would be excommunicated without exception (Pallen and Wynne

1929:149, 266). The missionaries who had arrived in Japan would have strictly prohibited cremation of the dead.

106. While these are violent deaths, they are nevertheless natural and thus do not prevent the body's resurrection.

107. The *Tenchi*, that is, forbids using mummies as medicine. The text employs the word *miira*, the Portuguese word for mummy, which entered the Japanese lexicon with the arrival of the Portuguese and Spanish in Japan in the mid-sixteenth century. Through them Japanese learned of the ancient Egyptian practice of mummification, in which myrrh (Port. *miira*) was essential in the preparation of the corpse. The Japanese themselves had practiced a form of self-mummification since the eleventh century, although myrrh was not an ingredient and the ideological basis for this practice was completely different from the Egyptian. The Japanese practice had strong links with the Maitreya faith, a messianic form of Buddhism that rested on the belief in the coming of the future Buddha. In order to assist Maitreya, they wanted to meet him in their human form and as mummies they could achieve this. Practitioners would eliminate all cereal crops from their diet and consume only fruit and berries until their bodies withered and the internal organs rotted (Cockburn and Cockburn 1983:211–223; Raveri 1992:8).

The mummies referred to in this passage, however, have nothing in common with self-mummification or religious practice. Instead the Kakure Kirishitan are referring to mummies imported to Japan from Europe, where the use of mummies as medicine had become widespread. According to three Japanese sources of the seventeenth century, mummies were brought into Japan by Western merchants. The following works describe the use of mummies as medicine: *Ihō Kuketsu* (Oral Secrets of Medical Technique) by Nagasawa Dōju (1681); *Yamato Honzō Hisei* (The Correct Japanese Pharmacopoeia), a reedition of a work by Kaibara Ekiken (1709); and *Kōmōdan* (Chats on Red Hair) by Gotō Rishun (1765). These works describe how mummies were acquired abroad, the trafficking in "counterfeit" mummies, and the virtues of mummy medicine itself. The most common method of preparation was to grind pieces of mummy into a powder, mix the powder with liquid, and then drink it as a tonic. The medicine seems to have been efficacious in the treatment of bruises and wounds. (The asphalt and bitumen in the mummy helped heal broken and lacerated veins.) According to the sources mentioned above, whole mummies were brought to Japan by the Dutch after they supplanted the Portuguese in trade. By this time Japanese had begun to make their own imitation mummies.

While the importation of mummies to Japan may appear sensational, mummy medicine had had a long history in the West since about 1100. Not until the sixteenth and seventeenth centuries, however, did it become a common drug in European apothecaries. The rich profits that accrued from traffic in mummies eventually encouraged a certain unscrupulous entrepreneurism: searching Egyptian tombs, stealing the mummies, and breaking them into small pieces were practices that had caught the notice of Egyptian officials, who finally forbade the export of mummies. This restriction in turn gave rise to the sordid practice of making counterfeit mummies acquired by dubious means. Several accounts state that use was made of executed criminals, slaves, or the bodies of travelers lost in the desert. By filling them with asphaltum, stitching them up, and drying them in the sun, they were passable as ancient Egyptian mummies. Ultimately the traffic in mummies ceased owing to the discovery of numerous frauds among mummy merchants (Pettigrew 1834:7–12). For a fictional account of mummy trafficking, see Shibusawa Tatsuhiko's *Takaoka Shinnō Kōkai-ki* (Record of the Voyage of Prince Takaoka): the chapter titled "The Honeyman" refers to the practice of gathering up the bodies of travelers lost in the desert to sell as mummies.

That the Kakure Kirishitan living in and around Nagasaki knew of this mummy medicine is not surprising, since this was the only open port in the country. Their condemnation of the medicine, clearly stated in the *Tenchi,* is consistent with their attitude toward the human body. Consumption of such medicine would indeed interfere with the mummified body's chance of resurrection.

108. The expression here is *hottai o ukeru,* a Buddhist expression meaning "to become a buddha."

109. Ammei Zesusu (Lat. "Amen, Iesu") is a traditional way to end a prayer. Here it ends the entire sacred text of the *Tenchi Hajimari no Koto*.

110. Meido (Dark World) is a Buddhist term that refers to the world where all people must go after death. In Meido ten judges will judge the past sins of the deceased. Each judgment is presided over by one of the specialist judges and pertains to a period after death. Thus the seventh day after death is the first judgment. These judgments continue periodically for three years, by which time the soul has been thoroughly examined. It is then sent to the appropriate heaven. Thus Meido is a kind of vestibule where the soul must await its judgment.

111. Santosu-sama (Port. *Santo*): "the saint."

****

Bibliography

Amann, Émile. *Le Protévangile de Jacques et Ses Remaniements Latins.* Paris: Letouzey et Ane Editeurs, 1910.

Anesaki Masaharu. *The Mythology of All Races: Japan.* Vol. 13. Boston: Marshall Jones, 1928.

———. "Writings on Martyrdom in Kirishitan Literature." *Transactions of the Asiatic Society of Japan* 8(1931):20–65.

Aston, W. G., trans. *Nihongi: Chronicles of Japan from the Earliest Times to* A.D. *697.* Tokyo: Tuttle, 1972.

Bellah, Robert. *Tokugawa Religion: The Roots of Modern Japan.* New York: Macmillan, 1985.

Berger, Peter. *Invitation to Sociology: A Humanistic Perspective.* New York: Doubleday, 1963.

———. *A Rumor of Angels: Modern Society and the Rediscovery of the Supernatural.* New York: Doubleday, 1969.

Blacker, Carmen. *The Catalpa Bow: A Study of Shamanistic Practices in Japan.* London: Allen & Unwin, 1975.

Bohner, Alfred. "Tenchi Hajimari no Koto: Wie Himmel und Erde Entstanden." *Monumenta Nipponica* 1(2)(1938):465–514.

Bolle, Kees W., ed. *Secrecy in Religion.* Lieden: Brill, 1987.

Boxer, Charles. *The Christian Century in Japan 1549–1650.* Berkeley: University of California Press, 1951.

———. "The Clandestine Catholic Church in Feudal Japan: 1614–1640." *History Today* 16(1966):53–61.

Brodrick, James, S.J. *The Progress of the Jesuits (1556–1579).* New York: Longmans, 1947.

Cardenal, Ernesto. *The Gospel in Solentiname.* Vol. 2. New York: Orbis, 1985.

Carletti, Francesco. *My Voyage Around the World.* Translated by Herbert Weinstock. London: Methuen, 1965.

Carroll, Michael P. *Madonnas That Maim: Popular Catholicism in Italy Since the Fifteenth Century.* Baltimore: Johns Hopkins University Press, 1992.

Cary, Otis. *A History of Christianity in Japan.* Tokyo: Tuttle, 1976.

Casal, U. A. "Japanese Cosmetics and Teethblackening." *Transactions of the Asiatic Society of Japan,* 3rd series, 9(1966):5–27.

Catechism of the Catholic Church. London: Geoffrey Chapman, 1994.

Christian, William A., Jr. *Local Religion in Sixteenth-Century Spain.* Princeton: Princeton University Press, 1981a.

———. *Apparitions in Late Medieval and Renaissance Spain.* Princeton: Princeton University Press, 1981b.

———. *Moving Crucifixes in Modern Spain.* Princeton: Princeton University Press, 1992.

Cieslik, Hubert, S.J. *Kirishitan jidai no hōjin shisai* キリシタン時代の 邦人司祭 (Japanese priests of the Christian era). Kirishitan Bunka Kenkyū Shiriizu 22. Tokyo: Sophia University, キリシタン文化研 究シリーズ 1981.

Cirlot, J. E. *A Dictionary of Symbols.* New York: Routledge & Kegan Paul, 1978.

Cockburn, Aidan, and Eve Cockburn. *Mummies, Disease, and Ancient Cultures.* Cambridge: Cambridge University Press, 1983.

Cooper, Michael. *They Came to Japan: An Anthology of European Reports on Japan 1543–1640.* Berkeley: University of California Press, 1965.

———. *The Southern Barbarians.* Tokyo: Kodansha, 1971.

———. *Rodrigues the Interpreter: An Early Jesuit in Japan and China.* New York: Weatherhill, 1974.

———. "Christianity." In *Kodansha Encyclopedia.* Tokyo: Kodansha, 1983.

———. "The Early Jesuits and Buddhism." *Renaissance Institute.* Tokyo: Sophia University, 1994.

Cullman, O. "Infancy Gospels." In *New Testament Apocrypha: Gospels and Related Writings,* vol. 1, ed. E. Hennecke and W. Schneemelcher. Cambridge: Lutterworth, 1973.

Dale, Peter. *The Myth of Japanese Uniqueness.* New York: St. Martin's Press, 1988.

Delgado García, José, O.P. "Koshikijima no Kakure Kirishitan" 甑島

の隠れ切支丹. *Kirishitan Bunka Kenkyū-kai Kaihō* キリシタン文化研究会会報 25(3)(Dec. 1985a):67–69.

———. *El Beato Francisco Morales O.P. Mártir de Japón (1567–1622): Su personalidad histórica y misionera.* Madrid: Instituto Pontificio de Teologia/Misionologia, 1985b.

De Montfort, Louis. *The Secret of the Rosary.* New York: Montfort Publications, 1991.

De Visser, M. W. "The Tengu." *Transactions of the Asiatic Society of Japan* 36(2)(1908):25–99.

De Vries, A. D. *Dictionary of Symbols and Imagery.* New York: North Holland, 1974.

Dictionary of Buddhist Terms and Concepts. Tokyo: Nichiren Shōshū International Center, 1983.

Dorson, Richard, ed. *Studies in Japanese Folklore.* Bloomington: Indiana University Press, 1963.

Drummond, Richard Henry. *A History of Christianity in Japan.* Grand Rapids: Eerdmans, 1971.

Dumas, François Ribandeau. *Grandeur et Misère des Jésuites.* Paris: Les Productions de Paris, 1963.

Earhart, Byron H. *Religions of Japan: Many Traditions Within One Sacred Way.* San Francisco: Harper, 1984.

Ebisawa Arimichi 海老沢有道. *Keiki Kirishitan Shiwa: Nihonjin Iruman Rorenso no Sokuseki o tadoritsutsu* 京幾切支丹史話, 日本人伊留満ロセンソの足跡を辿つつ (History of the Christians of Kyoto and Osaka: Tracing the footsteps of Brother Lourenço). Tokyo: Tōkyōdō, 1942a.

———. "Irmão Lourenço: The First Japanese Lay-Brother of the Society of Jesus and His Letter." *Monumenta Nipponica* 5(1)(1942b): 225–233.

———. "Confraria." *Seishin Joshi Daigaku Ronsō* 聖心女子大学論叢 (Seishin Studies) 8(1956):65–92.

———. "Crypto-Christianity in Tokugawa Japan." *Japan Quarterly* 7(1960):288–294.

———. "Dochiriina Kirishitan" どちりいなキリシタン. In *Kirishitan-sho, Haiya-sho* キリシタン書排耶書 (Kirishitan and Anti-Kirishitan writings). Nihon Shisō Taikei 日本思想大系 (Collection of Japanese thought). Tokyo: Iwanami Shoten, 1970a.

———. "Tenchi Hajimari no Koto" 天地始之事. In *Kirishitan-sho, Haiya-sho.* Tokyo: Iwanami Shoten, 1970b.

Edel, Chantal, and Linda Coverdale. *Once Upon a Time: Visions of Old Japan*. Photographs by Felice Beato and Baron Raimund von Stillfried. New York: Friendly Press, 1986.

Eder, Matthias. "Reality in Japanese Folktales." *Asian Folklore Studies* 28(1)(1969):17–26.

Elison, George. *Deus Destroyed: The Image of Christianity in Early Modern Japan*. Cambridge: Harvard University Press, 1988.

Embree, John. *Suye-mura, a Japanese Village*. Chicago: University of Chicago Press, 1939.

Endō Shūsaku 遠藤周作. *Kirishitan no Sato* キリシタンの里 (Christian village). Tokyo: Jinbun Shoin, 1941.

———. *Kirishitan Jidai: Junkyō to kikyō no rekishi* 切支丹の時代：殉教と棄教の歴史 (Kirishitan era: A history of martyrdom and apostasy). Tokyo: Shōgakkan raiburarii, 1994.

England, John. "The Earliest Christian Communities in Southeast and Northeast Asia: An Outline of the Evidence Available in Seven Countries Before A.D. 1500." *Missiology* (April 1991): 203–215.

———. "The Hidden History of Christianity in Asia: The Churches of the East Before 1500 C.E." In *Doing Theology with Asian Resources*, ed. Archie C. C. Lee. Auckland: Pace, 1993.

Fabella, Virginia. *Asian Christian Spirituality: Reclaiming Traditions*. New York: Orbis, 1992.

Fouqueray, Le P. Henri, S.J. *Histoire de la Compagnie de Jésus en France des Origines á la Suppression (1528–1762)*. Vol. 1. Paris: Librairie Alphonse Picard et Fils, 1910.

Frois, Luis P., S.J. *Historia de Japam*. 5 vols. Edited by José Wicki, S.J. Lisbon: Biblioteca Nacional, 1984.

Fukagata Hisashi 深潟久. "Sotome Monogatari: Hyōryū Suru Shinkō" 外海物語：漂流する信仰 (Story of Sotome: Drifting beliefs). In *Sotome-chō: Kirishitan no Sato* 外海町, キリシタンの里 (Sotome: A Christian village). Sotome: Sotome-chō Yakuba, 1983.

Furuno Kiyoto 古野清人. *Kakure Kirishitan* 隠れキリシタン (Hidden Christians of Japan). Tokyo: Shibundō, 1984.

Ginzburg, Carlo. *I Benandanti: La Stregonaria e Culti Agrari tra Cinquecento e Seicento*. Turin: Einaudi, 1972.

———. *Il Formaggio e i Vermi: Il Cosmo di un Mugnaio del '500*. Turin: Einaudi, 1976.

Gonoi Takashi 後野井隆史. *Tokugawa Shoki Kirishitanshi Kenkyū*

徳川初期キリシタン史研究 (Study in early Christian history). Tokyo: Yoshikawa Kōbunkan, 1983.

———. *Nihon Kirisutokyō-shi* 日本キリスト教史 (Japanese Christian history). Tokyo: Yoshikawa Kōbunkan, 1990.

Gotō Rishun 後藤光生. *Bunmei Genryū Sōsho* 文明源流叢書 (Original Civilization Series). Vol. 1: *Kōmōdan* 紅毛談 (1765) (Chats on red hair). Tokyo: Meicho kankōkai, 1969.

Gubbins, John H. "Review of *The Introduction of Christianity into China and Japan.*" *Transactions of the Asiatic Society of Japan* 6(1)(1877–1878):1–62.

Gunke Shinichi 郡家真一. *Gotō Hōgen-shū* 五島方言集 (Glossary of the Gotō dialect). Tokyo: Kokusho kankōkai, 1931.

Hall, James. *Seiyō Bijutsu Kaidoku Jiten* 西洋美術解読事典. (Originally published as *Hall's Dictionary of Subjects and Symbols in Art.*) Tokyo: Kawade shobō shinsha, 1990.

Harrington, Ann M. *Japan's Hidden Christians.* Chicago: Loyola University Press, 1993.

Hartmann, Arnulf, O.S.A. *The Augustinians in Seventeenth Century Japan.* New York: Augustinian Historical Institute, 1965.

Hashiura Yasuo 橋浦泰雄. *Gotō minzoku zushi* 五島民俗図誌 (Gotō ethnographical documents). Tokyo: Kokusho kankōkai, 1974.

Hemphill, Elizabeth Anne. *The Least of These: Miki Sawada and Her Children.* New York: Weatherhill, 1980.

Hori Ichirō. *Folk Religion of Japan.* Midway Reprint. Chicago: University of Chicago Press, 1968.

Inada Kōji 稲田浩二. *Nihon Mukashibanashi Tsūkan* 日本昔話通観 (General survey and analysis of Japanese folktales). Vol. 28: *Mukashibanashi taipu indekusu* 昔話タイプインデックス (A type-index of folktales). Kyoto: Doshosha, 1988.

Iwamura Mitsuzō 岩村光蔵. "Warera no Shūkyō" 我等ノ宗教 (Our religion). English translation by Christal Whelan and Ben Ishii. Unpublished manuscript, 1972.

Japanese Religion: A Survey by the Agency for Cultural Affairs. New York: Kodansha, 1990.

Jennes, Joseph, C.I.C.M. *A History of the Catholic Church in Japan: From Its Beginnings to the Early Meiji Era.* Tokyo: Oriens Institute for Religious Research, 1973.

Jōdo Shinshū Seiten 浄土真宗聖典 (Sacred book of the Jōdo Shin sect). Kyoto: Honganji shuppan, 1988.

Kaempfer, Engelbert. *The History of Japan Together with a Description of the Kingdom of Siam.* Vols. 2–3. Glasgow: James Mac-Lehose & Sons, 1906.

Kaibara Ekiken 貝原益軒. *Ekiken Zenshū* 益軒全集 (Complete works of Ekiken Kaibara). Vol. 6. Tokyo: Ekiken-shū kankōbu, 1910–1911.

Kamiya Takehiro 紙谷威広. *Kirishitan no Shinwa-Teki Sekai* キリシタンの神話的世界 (The Mythological World of the Christians). Tokyo: Tōkyōdō shuppan, 1986.

Kataoka Yakichi 片岡弥吉. "Kakure kirishitan" かくれキリシタン. In *Kinsei no chika shinkō* 近世の地下信仰 (Modern hidden beliefs), edited by Kataoka et al. Tokyo: Hyōronsha, 1966.

————. *Kakure Kirishitan: Rekishi to Minzoku* 隠れキリシタン：歴史と民俗 (The history and folkways of the Kakure Kirishitan). Tokyo: Nihon hōsō shuppan kyōkai, 1967.

————. *Nihon Kirishitan Junkyō-shi* 日本キリシタン殉教史 (A history of Japanese martyrdom). Tokyo: Jiji Tsūshinsha, 1979.

————. *Fumi-e: Kinkyō no Rekishi* 踏絵：禁教の歴史 (*Fumi-e:* History of a prohibited religion). Tokyo: Nihon hōsō shuppan kyōkai, 1981.

Kawaguchi Zennosuke 川口善之助. *Kakure Kirishitan Orasshio no Shiori* 隠れ切支丹オラッシオのしおり (Guide to the Hidden Christian Orasshio). Nagasaki: Kakure kirishitan kenkyūkai, 1954.

Kawai Hayao 河合隼雄. "Monogatari ni Miru Tōyō to Seiyō" 物語にみる東洋と西洋 (East and West as seen in tales). In *Monogatari to Ningen no Kagaku* 物語と人間の科学 (The science of people and their tales). Tokyo: Iwanami shoten, 1993.

Ketelaar, James Edward. *Of Heretics and Martyrs in Meiji Japan: Buddhism and Its Persecution.* Princeton: Princeton University Press, 1990.

Kitagawa, Joseph. *On Understanding Japanese Religions.* Princeton: Princeton University Press, 1987.

————. *Religion in Japanese History.* New York: Columbia University Press, 1990.

Kojima Yukie 小島幸枝. "Tenchi Hajimari no Koto no Goi no Shūhen" 「天地始之事」の語彙の周辺 (The parameters of vocabulary in the *Tenchi Hajimari no Koto*). *Kirishitan Bunka Kenkyū Kaihō* キリシタン文化研究会報 (Bulletin of research on Kirishitan culture) 2(3)(Feb. 1969):72–80.

Konjaku Monogatari-shū 2 今昔物語集 (Konjaku monogatari collection). *Nihon Koten Bungaku Taikei* 日本古典文学大系 (Outline of classical Japanese literature). Tokyo: Iwanami shoten, 1960.

Kudamatsu Kazunori 久田松和則. *Ōmura-shi: Kinko Jitsugetsu* 大村史：琴湖の日月 (History of Ōmura: Passage of time at Lake Kin). Tokyo: Kokusho kankōkai, 1989.

Lauf, Detlef Ingo. *Secret Doctrines of the Tibetan Books of the Dead.* Boston: Shambhala, 1986.

Laures, Johannes, S.J. *Kirishitan Bunko: A Manual of Books and Documents on the Early Christian Mission in Japan.* 3rd ed. Tokyo: Sophia University, 1957.

Long, Charles. *Alpha: Myths of Creation.* New York: Collier Books, 1963.

Longnon, Jean, and Raymond Cazelles. *Die Très Riches Heures des Jean Duc de Berry im Musée Condé Chantilly.* Munich: Prestel-Verlag, 1973.

López Gay, Jesús, S.J. *El Catecumenando en la mission del Japon del S. XVI.* Rome: Libreria dell'Università Gregoriana, 1966.

Marnas, Francisque, M.A. *La Religion de Jésus resuscitée au Japon dans la seconde moitié du XIXe siècle.* Vol. 1. Paris-Lyon: Delhomme et Briguet, 1896.

Matsuda Kiichi 松田毅一. *Nanban no Bateren* 南蛮のバテレン (The Southern Barbarian priests). Tokyo: Chōbunsha, 1993.

Mayer, Fanny Hagin, trans. *The Yanagita Kunio Guide to the Japanese Folk Tale.* Bloomington: Indiana University Press, 1948.

Mazzali, Ettore, ed. *Milione.* By Marco Polo. Milan: Garzanti, 1982.

McGrath, Alister E. *Christian Theology: An Introduction.* Oxford: Blackwell, 1994.

Metford, J.C.J. *Dictionary of Christian Lore and Legend.* London: Thames & Hudson, 1983.

Minzokugaku kenkyūjo 民俗学研究所 (Folklore Research Institute). *Kaitei Sōgō Nippon Minzoku Goi* 改訂綜合日本民俗語彙 (Revised comprehensive folklore glossary). Vol. 2. Tokyo: Heibonsha, 1955.

Missions-Etrangères, Comptes Rendus 1878. Seminaire des Missions-Etrangères, Lettre Commune 9. Paris, 31 December 1878.

Mitford, A. B. [Lord Redesdale]. *Tales of Old Japan.* London: Macmillan, 1871.

Miyazaki Kentarō 宮崎賢太郎. " 'Tenchi Hajimari no Koto' kō" 「天地始之事」考 (Thoughts on the *Tenchi Hajimari no Koto*).

Nagasaki Chihō Bunkashi Kenkyū 長崎地方文化史研究 (Nagasaki studies in the history of culture) 4 (1988).

———. "Ikitsuki Kakure Kirishitan no Nodachi no Gyōji Kenkyū" 生月カクレキリシタンの「野立ち」の行事研究 (A study of the "Nodachi Rite" of the Kakure Kirishitan of Ikitsuki Island). *Nagasaki Junshin Joshi Tanki Daigaku Kiyō* 長崎純心女子短期大学紀要 (Proceedings of Nagasaki Junshin Women's College) 27(1991):33–52.

———. "Hidden Christians in Contemporary Nagasaki." *Crossroads* (Nagasaki) 1(Summer 1993):35–45.

Moffett, Samuel Hugh. *A History of Christianity in Asia*. Vol. 1: *Beginnings to 1500*. San Francisco: Harper, 1992.

Morita Kiyoko. *The Book of Incense*. Tokyo: Kodansha, 1992.

Nagasawa Dōju 長沢道寿. *Ihō Kuketsu Shū 1681* 医方口訣集 1681 (Collection of oral secrets of medicinal technique, 1681). Facsimile ed. Tokyo: Meicho shuppan, 1982.

Naitō Michio 内藤道雄. "Kakure kirishitan to Mōzaruto" 隠れキリシタンとモージァルト (The Hidden Christians and Mozart). *Brunnen* (Tokyo) 361(March 1994):3–5.

Nakajima Isao 中島功. *Gotō Hennen-shi* 五島編年史 (Annals of Gotō). Vol. 2. Tokyo: Kokusho Kankōkai, 1973.

Naru-chō Kikaku-Zaiseika 奈留町企画財政課 (Narushima Section for Financial Planning). *Don Don Naru* ドンドン奈留 (Forward Naru). Narushima, 1993.

Naru-chō Kyōiku Iinkai 奈留町教育委員会. *Kyōdo Naru* 郷土奈留 (Local lore of Naru). Nagasaki: Naru-chō Kyōiku Iinkai 1973; 1992.

New English Bible with the Apocrypha. Oxford: Oxford University Press, 1972.

Nihon Kirisutokyō Rekishi Daijiten 日本キリスト教歴史大事典 (Dictionary of Japanese Christian history). Tokyo: Kyobunkan, 1988.

Nihon Miira Kenkyū Gurūpu 日本ミイラ研究グループ (Group for research on Japanese mummies). *Nihon-Chūgoku Miira Shinkō no Kenkyū* 日本中国ミイラ信仰の研究 (Mummy worship in Japan and China). Tokyo: Heibonsha, 1993.

Nippon Hōsō Shuppan Kyōkai 日本放送出版協会. "Yuki no Santa Maria: Ruten no Nanban Eshitachi" 雪のサンタ・マリア流転の南蛮絵師たち (The wanderings of Southern Barbarian painters). In

Rekishi Dokyumento 歴史ドキュメント (Historical documents). Tokyo: NHK, 1987.

Nippon Shūkyō Jiten 日本宗教辞典 (Dictionary of Japanese religions). Tokyo: Kobundō, 1985.

Nosco, Peter. "Secrecy and the Transmission of Tradition: Issues in the Study of the 'Underground' Christians." *Japanese Journal of Religious Studies* 20(1993):1–29.

Ōkawa Essei 大川悦生. *Nihon no Densetsu: Minami Nihonhen* 日本の伝説：南日本編 (Japanese legends: Southern Japan). Tokyo: Kaiseisha, 1978.

Ono Sokyo. *Shinto: The Kami Way*. Tokyo: Tuttle, 1990.

Ōno Yūji 大野祐二. "Girei to Shakai Henka: Gotō Rettō Narushima no Jirei Kenkyū" 儀礼と社会変化：五島列島奈留島の事例研究 (Ritual and social change: A case study on Narushima, Gotō Islands). Unpublished master's thesis, Komazawa University, Tokyo, 1989.

Ozaki, Yei Theodora. *The Japanese Fairy Book*. Tokyo: Tuttle, 1970.

Paglia, Camille. *Sexual Personae: Art and Decadence from Nefertiti to Emily Dickinson*. New Haven: Yale University Press, 1990.

Pallen, Conde B., and John J. Wynne. *The New Catholic Dictionary*. New York: Universal Knowledge Foundation, 1929.

Paske-Smith, Montague. *Japanese Traditions of Christianity: Being Some Old Translations from the Japanese, with British Consular Reports of the Persecutions of 1868–1872*. Kobe: L. Thompson & Co., 1929.

Perrin, Noel. *Giving Up the Gun: Japan's Reversion to the Sword 1543–1879*. Boston: Godine, 1979.

Petitjean, Bernard. "Seikyō Shogaku Yōri" 聖教初学要理 (A fundamental catechism of Christian doctrine). In *Meiji Bunka Zenshū* 明治文化全集 (Collection of works on Meiji culture). Vol. 11. Tokyo: Nippon hyōronsha, 1928.

Pettigrew, Thomas Joseph. *History of Egyptian Mummies*. London: Longman, 1834.

Philippi, Donald. *Kojiki*. Translation and commentary. Tokyo: Tokyo University Press, 1989.

Pieris, Aloysius, S.J. *An Asian Theology of Liberation*. New York: Orbis, 1988.

Puebla Pedrosa, Ceferino, O.P. *Witnesses of the Faith in the Orient:*

Dominican Martyrs of Japan, China, and Vietnam. Hong Kong: Dominican Missions, 1989.

Rapoport, Louis. "The Origins of Ethiopian Jewry." *Jerusalem Post,* 26 May 1991, p. 14.

Raveri, Massimo. *Il Corpo e Il Paradiso: Esperienze Ascetiche in Asia Orientale.* Venice: Saggi Marsilio, 1992.

Raz, Jacob. *Aspects of Otherness in Japanese Culture.* Tokyo: Institute for the Study of Languages and Cultures of Asia and Africa, Tokyo University of Foreign Studies, 1992.

Reader, Ian. *Religion in Contemporary Japan.* Honolulu: University of Hawai'i Press, 1991.

Roth, Cecil. *Los Judios Secretos: Historia de los Marranos.* Madrid: Altalena, 1979.

Ruch, Barbara. "Medieval Jongleurs and the Making of a National Literature." In *Japan in the Muromachi Age.* Berkeley: University of California Press, 1977.

Ryan, William Granger. *The Golden Legend: Readings on the Saints.* Vol. 1. Princeton: Princeton University Press, 1993.

Saeki, P. Y. "The Nestorian Relics in Japan." In *The Nestorian Documents and Relics in China.* Tokyo: Maruzen, 1937.

Schull, William J. "The Effect of Christianity on Consanguinity in Nagasaki." *American Anthropologist* 55(1953):74–89.

———. "Kuroshima: The Impact of Religion on an Island's Genetic Heritage." *Human Biology* 34(1962):271–298.

Schurhammer, Georg, S.J. *Francis Xavier: His Life, His Times.* Vol. 4: *Japan and China 1549–1552.* Rome: Jesuit Historical Institute, 1982.

Schütte, J. F., S.J. "Christliche Japanische Literatur, Bilder und Druckblätter in einem unbekannten Vatikanischen Codex aus dem Jahre 1591." *Archivum Historicum Societatis Iesu,* vol. 10. Rome, 1940.

———. "Regimento Pera os Semynarios de Japan 1580." *Valignanos Missionsgrundsätze für Japan.* Vol. 1, pt. 2: 1580–1582. Rome: Edizioni de Storia e Letteratura, 1958.

———. "Bachikan toshokanzō Bareto shahon ni tsuite" ヴァチカン図書館蔵バレト写本について (The Barreto Manuscript in the Vatican Collection). *Kirishitan Kenkyū,* vol. 7. Tokyo: Yoshikawa kōbunkan, 1962.

———. *Introductio ad Historiam Societatis Iesu in Japonia (1549–1650).* Rome: Historical Institute of the Society of Jesus, 1968.

————. *Monumenta Missionium Societatis Iesu: Missiones Orientales Monumenta Historica, Japoniae I (1553–1614)*. Vol. 34. Rome: Societatis Iesu, 1975.

Shibusawa Tatsuhiko 渋沢龍彦. *Takaoka Shinnō Kōkaiki* 高丘親王航海記 (Record of the voyage of Prince Takaoka). Tokyo: Bungei shunjū, 1988.

Shirayanagi Seiichi. *Romaji-Eibun Atarashii Missa no Shiki Shidai* (The order of the Mass). Tokyo: Enderle Book Co., 1971.

Sōgō Bukkyō daijiten 総合佛教大辞典 (Comprehensive Buddhist dictionary). Vol. 3. Kyoto: Hōzōkan, 1987.

Spence, Jonathan. *The Memory Palace of Matteo Ricci*. New York: Penguin, 1984.

Suzuki Hiromitsu 鈴木広光. "Kirishitan Shūkyōsho ni okeru Bukkyōgo mondai" キリシタン宗教書における仏教語問題 (Problems concerning Buddhist words in Kirishitan religious books). *Nagoya Daigaku Bungakubu Kenkyū Ronshū* 名古屋大学文学部研究論集 (Nagoya University's Literature Research Notes) 109(37)(March 1991):1–12.

Tagita Kōya 田北耕也. "Tenchi Hajimari no Koto." *Katorikku-shi* カトリック誌 (Studies in Catholicism) 18(3)(1938):94–115 and 4:101–120; 19(1)(1939):69–88 and 2:108–132.

————. "Study of Acculturation Among the Secret Christians of Japan." *Nagoya Joshi Shōka Tanki Daigaku Kiyō* 名古屋女子商科短期大学紀要 (Journal of Nagoya Women's Junior College of Commerce) 1(Oct. 1965):141–158; 2(April 1966):124–139; 3(Oct. 1966):96–123; 4(April 1967):62–86.

————. "Meeting of Religions in the Tenchi Hajimari no Koto." *Dōhō Gakuhō* 同朋学報 (Dōhō University Bulletin) 16(1967):3–9.

————. *Shōwa jidai no senpuku kirishitan* 昭和時代の潜伏キリシタン (Secret Christians of the Shōwa era). 3rd ed. Tokyo: Kokusho kankōkai, 1978.

Tanaka Yōjirō 田中用次郎. "Yuki no Santa Maria" 雪のサンタ・マリア (Our Lady of the Snow). *Katorikku seikatsu* カトリック生活 (Catholic life) 5(660)(1984):9–11.

Tani Shinsuke 谷真介. *Kirishitan Densetsu Hyakuwa* キリシタン伝説百話 (Collection of Kirishitan legends). Tokyo: Shinchō sensho, 1987.

Tanigawa Ken'ichi 谷川健一. "Watashi no *Tenchi Hajimari no Koto*" わたしの「天地始之事」 (My "Beginning of Heaven and Earth").

Tanigawa Ken'ichi Chosaku-shū 谷川健一著作集 (Collected works of Tanigawa Ken'ichi), vol. 10. Tokyo: Sanichi shobō, 1986.

Tedlock, Dennis. "Torture in the Archives: Mayans Meet Europeans." *American Anthropologist* 95(1)(1993):139–152.

Tsuruda Yasunari 鶴田八洲也. *Saikai no Kirishitan Bunka Sōran* 西海のキリシタン文化綜覧 (A general survey of the culture of the Kirishitan of the Western Sea area). Hondo: Amakusa bunka shuppansha, 1983.

Turnbull, Stephen. "From Catechist to Kami: Martyrs and Mythology Among the Kakure Kirishitan." *Japanese Religions* 19(1–2)(1994): 58–81.

———. "Mass or Matsuri: The Oyashiki-sama Ceremony on Ikitsuki." *Monumenta Nipponica* 50(2)(1995):171–188.

———. "Acculturation among the Kakure Kirishitan: Some conclusions from the *Tenchi Hajimari no Koto.*" In *Japan and Christianity: Impacts and Responses*, edited by John Breen and Mark Williams. London: Macmillan, 1996.

Urakawa Wasaburō 浦河和三郎. *Gotō Kirishitan-shi* 五島キリシタン史 (A Christian history of Gotō). Tokyo: Kokusho Kankōkai, 1973.

———. *Kirishitan no Fukkatsu* 切支丹の復活 (Revival of the Christians in Japan). Tokyo: Kokusho Kankōkai, 1979.

Uyttenbroeck, Thomas, O.F.M. *Early Franciscans in Japan.* Missionary Bulletin Series, no. 6. Himeji: Himeji Japanese Committee of the Apostolate, 1958.

Van Wolferen, Karel. *The Enigma of Japanese Power.* London: Macmillan, 1990.

Volpe, Angela. *I Kakure: Religione e Società in Giappone.* Reggio Emilia: One Way, 1992.

Von Franz, Marie-Louise. *An Introduction to the Interpretation of Fairytales.* Irving, Texas, and Zurich: Spring Publications, 1973.

Wauchope, Robert. *Lost Tribes and Sunken Continents: Myth and Method in the Study of American Indians.* Chicago: University of Chicago Press, 1962.

Weaver, Mary Jo. *New Catholic Women: A Contemporary Challenge to Traditional Religious Authority.* New York: Harper & Row, 1985.

Whelan, Christal. "Religion Concealed: The Kakure Kirishitan on Narushima." *Monumenta Nipponica* 47(3)(1992):369–387.

———. "Loss of the Signified Among the Kakure Kirishitan." *Japanese Religions* 19(1–2)(1994a):82–105.

———. "Japan's Vanishing Minority: The Kakure Kirishitan of the Gotō Islands." *Japan Quarterly* 41(4)(1994b):434–449.

Whone, Herbert. *Church, Monastery, Cathedral: A Guide to the Symbolism of the Christian Tradition.* New Jersey: Ridley Enslow, 1977.

Wilson, Bryan. *Sects and Society.* London: Heinemann, 1961.

Yanagita Kunio 柳田国男. "Kōraijima no Densetsu" 高麗島の伝説 (The legend of Koraijima). In *Yanagita Kunio Zenshū* 柳田国男全集 (Collected works of Yanagita Kunio), vol. 1. Tokyo: Chikuma shobō, 1992.

Yoshimatsu Yūichi 吉松祐一. *Nagasaki no Minwa* 長崎の民話 (Folktales from Nagasaki), no. 48. Tokyo: Miraisha, 1981.

Yūki, Diego, S.J. *"Tenchi Hajimari no Koto."* *Nagasaki Dansō* 長崎談叢 (Topics on Nagasaki) 81(1994):1–26.

Broadcast Media

KTN Terebi Nagasaki KTNテレビ長崎 (KTN Television Nagasaki). *Kanashimi no agari itsu: Nagasaki no Kakure Kirishitan* 悲しみの上がりいつ：長崎の隠れキリシタン (When is Easter?: The Kakure Kirishitan of Nagasaki). 1984.

Terebi Nishi Nihon テレビ西日本 (Western Japan Television). *Nessa to hatō: Petoro Kibe no shōgai* 熱砂と波涛：ペトロ岐部の生涯 (Hot sands and rough seas: The life of Pedro Kibe). 1983.

Index

About the Translator

Christal Whelan is a lecturer in the Foreign Language Department at Sophia University in Tokyo. With a background in Portuguese and Italian literature and history, she came to Japan in 1990 to research the early contact between the Japanese and the Portuguese. In 1991 she spent eleven months living among the remnant of that early encounter—the Kakure Kirishitan (Hidden Christians)—in the remote Gotō Islands. Her research on Japanese religion has appeared in *Monumenta Nipponica, Japan Quarterly, Asian Folklore Studies,* and *Japanese Religions.* She is currently at work on a visual anthropology project to produce an ethno-documentary film on the Kakure Kirishitan of the Gotō Islands.